Introduction to the international money markets

~

KEITH REDHEAD
Principal Lecturer in Economics
Coventry Business School

Woodhead-Faulkner

NEW YORK   LONDON   TORONTO   SYDNEY
TOKYO   SINGAPORE

First published 1992 by
Woodhead-Faulkner (Publishers) Limited
Campus 400, Maylands Avenue
Hemel Hempstead
Hertfordshire, HP2 7EZ

A division of
Simon & Schuster International Group

Printed and bound in Great Britain by
T. J. Press (Padstow) Ltd., Padstow, Cornwall

British Library Cataloguing in Publication Data

A catalogue record for this book is available from
the British Library

ISBN 0-85941-730-1 (pbk)

3 4 5   98 97 96

Contents

Contents

Contents

Preface

Degree courses in financial economics and financial services have begun to proliferate in the 1990s. This reflects the growing importance of financial market analysis in both economics and business courses. Simultaneously the financial services sector has become more aware of the need for formal training in the area of financial markets, as evidenced by the emergence of the Securities Industry Examinations operated by the International Stock Exchange in London.

The existing literature in the area tends to be aimed at a fairly advanced level and is prone to be inaccessible to the beginner. The texts in existence typically assume an initial high level of understanding of economic theory and mathematical concepts. This reflects the tendency for financial markets to be dealt with only at final year undergraduate or postgraduate level.

There is a movement towards financial markets being considered at earlier stages of courses. There is thus a need for textbooks that do not assume substantial initial knowledge of economic theory and mathematics. Such textbooks would also meet the needs of non-economists who need to understand financial markets. This text has been written in order to help satisfy the need for a book that assumes no prior knowledge and is therefore accessible to the beginner but which provides a thorough understanding of the international money markets broadly defined.

I should like to thank Marjorie and Mamie for their hard work on word processors.

1

Introduction: the recent history of international money

Much of the post-1945 history of international money has centred upon the reserves of international liquidity held by national governments. International liquidity takes the form of reserve assets held by governments for the purpose of being able to finance trade. Such reserves are assets which governments are prepared to accept from each other in the settlement of debts. A currency, or any other form of asset, must be acceptable to potential recipients if it is to function as a form of international liquidity. Currency within a country cannot function unless sellers are willing to accept it as a means of payment. In exactly the same way, a currency can be treated as an international means of payment only if countries are willing to accept it in settlement of debts arising from trade. International liquidity takes four forms:

(a) foreign exchange, primarily US dollars,
(b) gold,
(c) the ability to borrow from the International Monetary Fund (IMF) and
(d) a form of international money created and distributed by the IMF, known as Special Drawing Rights (SDRs).

For any one month, quarter or year the balance of payments of a country will not balance. There will be either a deficit or a surplus. The former requires a depletion of reserves of international liquidity in order to pay for the excess of imports over exports, the latter involves an addition to the country's reserves.

The Bretton Woods system

The international monetary system that operated between the late 1940s and the early 1970s is often referred to as the Bretton Woods system. The Bretton Woods system had three main characteristics.

1

Recent history of international money

Firstly, each participant was expected to establish a par value for its currency and maintain the foreign exchange value of its currency within 1% of that par value. In effect, this was a system in which exchange rates were fixed against the US dollar. In its turn, the US dollar was fixed in value in terms of gold at US$35 per ounce. The US government was prepared to sell gold to, or buy gold from, other governments at $35 per ounce.

Secondly, the IMF was established. Its main function was to lend currency to a member country whose foreign exchange reserves had become insufficient to support the value of its own currency at the par value. A country having substantial resort to the IMF would have to agree to economic policy prescriptions from the IMF. The IMF obtains its currency holdings by means of subscriptions. These are payments from member countries. The size of a country's subscription quota depends upon the size of its economy. Three-quarters of the quota is payable in the country's own currency. The remaining quarter was originally payable in gold, it is now payable in US dollars.

Thirdly, although the Bretton Woods system was based on fixed exchange rates there was scope for changing those fixed rates. A country could alter the par value of its currency in the event of 'fundamental disequilibrium' (which was not defined). Formally the country required approval from the IMF, although this was not always sought. Countries tended to see currency realignment as a last resort and were not prone to frequent changes in par values.

In the late 1940s most currencies were not convertible. This typically meant that buyers and sellers of a currency had to transact with the country's central bank. In such a situation, the central bank could arbitrarily fix the price of the currency. When a country made its currency convertible, transactions did not have to involve the central bank. In such circumstances an alternative means of maintaining the par value of a currency was required.

When currencies are convertible, exchange rates are determined by demand and supply. In order to maintain currency prices at fixed levels (or within small bands around such levels) central banks must intervene in the currency markets by buying or selling in order to influence demand or supply.

Not only did the Bretton Woods system involve fixed exchange rates it also involved a fixed price of gold at US$35 per ounce. Again this price was maintained (by the US government) by buying or selling gold whenever market forces tended to push the price away from $35.

2

A liquidity shortage?

A liquidity shortage?

Restoration of currency convertibility, as planned in the Bretton Woods agreement, required governments to have adequate reserves of gold and US dollars with which to intervene in the currency markets. Up until the early 1960s, there was a general feeling that the reserves were insufficient (many countries restored convertibility in the late 1950s or early 1960s). This situation had arisen both from a rapid increase in the demand for reserves and from a sluggish growth in their supply.

The increase in demand had taken place largely as a result of an increasing volume of world trade and an increase in the prices at which goods and services were traded. But other factors were at work. First, world trade was becoming increasingly unstable, an instability which increased the frequency of unexpectedly large balance of payments deficits. Correspondingly, the reserves required as a contingency against such large deficits were greater. Second, 'hot money' was becoming increasingly important: this is money which is quickly switched between currencies in search of the highest interest rates or speculative gain. A country suddenly confronted with a large outflow of such hot money is faced with consequent large sales of its currency as the owners of the hot money attempt to use it to buy other currencies (this is a deficit on the capital account of the balance of payments). If the government of the country wishes to prevent the excess supply of its currency from bringing about a fall in its foreign exchange value, it must purchase the surplus with its reserves of international liquidity (that is, its reserves are used to finance a deficit on the capital account). Thus the increased importance of hot money necessitated an expansion of reserves.

While the need for reserves rose sharply their availability increased slowly. Until the 1960s gold accounted for most of the reserves of international liquidity held in the world. However, the official price of gold remained constant at US$35 an ounce between 1934 and 1971. The gold already in existence failed to rise in monetary value to keep pace with the rising prices of traded goods. Furthermore, the failure of the gold price to rise in line with other prices and costs meant that its production became decreasingly profitable. Consequently, the lower relative price of gold hindered its production. Thus, while both the quantity of goods traded, and their prices, rose rapidly the amount of gold available expanded at an inadequate rate whilst the price of gold remained at its 1934 level. The ratio of the value of gold held in reserves to the value of goods traded fell considerably.

3

Recent history of international money

However, by the early 1960s anxieties about inadequate holdings of reserves, particularly US dollars, abated. This was largely due to the US balance of payments deficits which had added considerably to other countries' holdings of dollars. One consequence of the accumulation of official dollar holdings was that by the early 1960s the US dollar liabilities overseas exceeded US gold holdings. So the United States was no longer in a position to convert all foreign offical (central bank) dollar holdings into gold at $35 per ounce.

The confidence problem

Additions to other countries' dollar holdings are dependent upon the United States running a balance of payments deficit. If the rest of the world is to accumulate dollars, the dollars must flow out of the US economy, and that requires a balance of payments deficit with the excess of payments over receipts being financed with dollars. This means of providing the world with foreign exchange reserves has two major defects. Firstly, the supply of reserves is determined by the US deficits and not by the world's need for reserves. Secondly, there is the confidence problem. When a country has a balance of payments deficit, confidence in its currency as a source of international liquidity diminishes. A country with a persistent balance of payments deficit is liable to devalue its currency. Therefore, other nations may be reluctant to hold their foreign exchange reserves in the form of that country's currency. The acceptability of the currency will have lessened along with confidence in the maintenance of its value in terms of other currencies. It can thus be seen that the balance of payments deficits that supply the currency simultaneously undermine the acceptability of that currency. The fall in acceptability offsets the increase in supply.

The worldwide shortage of international liquidity subsequently gave way to a surplus. The development of the surplus arose from an increase in the supply of reserves. The main factor causing a massive increase in the supply of dollars as international liquidity was the financing of the Vietnam war. The US government financed the war largely by recourse to the printing of money. As the monetarists predicted, this led after a year or two to an increase in the US rate of inflation and to massive balance of payments deficits, and so the late 1960s and early 1970s were marked by massive US deficits and correspondingly large flows of dollars into the foreign exchange holdings of other countries.

4

Development of the eurodollar market

The development of the eurodollar market

In response to the continuing balance of payments deficits and the excess of dollar liabilities (dollars held by foreign central banks) over US gold reserves, the US government took steps in an attempt to staunch the foreign accumulation of dollars. In 1963 and 1964 an Interest Equalization Tax was imposed on lenders of US dollars to foreigners. This was a withholding tax payable by the lender to the US government (and which would be reflected in higher rates charged to the borrowers). The intention was to reduce lending in US dollars to non-US residents. In 1965 the US government instituted the Foreign Credit Restraint Program, which involved setting quotas on the lending of US banks to US-based multinationals that were involved in direct investment outside the United States.

These two measures provided a strong impetus to the development of the eurodollar market. Eurodollars are dollar deposits in banks outside the United States (since 1981 some banks located in the United States have been able to consider themselves to be outside the country for the purposes of eurodollar dealing – such US provisions are referred to as International Banking Facilities).

A cheque drawn on a domestic US bank could be deposited in a bank outside the United States (London is the main centre for eurodollar business). The bank receiving the cheque would acquire an asset in the form of a dollar deposit with the US-based bank and a liability that consists of the dollar-denominated deposit now held by the depositor of the cheque. The bank may then lend the eurodollars thereby replacing the asset in the form of a dollar deposit at a US bank with an asset in the form of a debt on the part of the borrower of the money. The deposit in the US-based bank is transferred to another bank. This transfer is direct if the lending is to the other bank (such interbank lending is common in eurocurrency markets) and indirect if the recipient of the money that is lent deposits it with another eurobank. When eurodollars are lent in this way more eurodollar deposits are created (via banks having deposits in other banks or through non-bank clients depositing money). Although the eurodollar market is the largest eurocurrency market it is not the only one. There are euro markets in all major currencies (in particular eurodeutschmarks, euroyen, euro-Swiss francs and eurosterling). The prefix 'euro' is misleading since eurocurrency markets are located throughout the world (not just in Europe).

Recent history of international money

Following the Suez crisis of 1956 there was downward pressure on the pound sterling and the British monetary authorities experienced difficulty in keeping sterling within 1% of its par value. In consequence, the Bank of England prohibited external sterling loans. The view was that if foreigners had less sterling they would be less able to impart downward pressure on its exchange rate by selling it.

However, London merchant banks were heavily involved in providing sterling loans for the purpose of financing international trade. When they were prevented from lending pounds sterling they replaced the sterling loans with US dollar loans. These loans were financed by attracting dollar deposits by offering competitive interest rates. Thus the eurodollar market came into existence.

The eurodollar market received impetus to its growth from US government restrictions. The Interest Equalization Tax and the Foreign Credit Restraint Program helped to create a demand for eurodollar loans since they hindered borrowing from US sources. Further to these measures, the US Federal Reserve introduced Regulation Q which imposed a ceiling on interest rates payable on bank deposits. In the mid-to-late 1960s dollar interest rates rose above the ceiling, and as a result depositors moved from the domestic market to the euromarket since the latter, being outside the United States, was not subject to US regulations. Money deposited in the offshore branches of US banks was often immediately re-lent to the US parent bank. Shell branches were often opened in the Cayman Islands or the Bahamas. Although these shell branches were legally registered outside the United States, the business involved was actually handled on the bank's US premises.

Gold and Special Drawing Rights

In order to keep gold at US$35 per ounce, the United States, together with the major European countries, established the gold pool in the early 1960s. As a group (via the Bank of England) they intervened in the gold market with a view to maintaining the dollar price of gold.

In the mid-1960s France converted substantial quantities of its dollar holdings into gold and in 1967 withdrew from the gold pool. Later in 1967, the pound was devalued. This raised the spectre of a possible dollar devaluation and consequently led to large-scale purchases of gold in order to transfer assets from dollars to gold. This put enormous strain on the gold pool (which sold huge quantities of gold) and in 1968 the control

6

of the private market price of gold was abandoned. A two-tier system for the price of gold began. Central banks were to transfer gold amongst themselves at $35 per ounce but would not trade in the private market. The private market was to trade at market-determined prices and there would be no central bank intervention. (The fixed official price of gold was abandoned in 1973.)

Special Drawing Rights (SDRs) are a form of internationally created money. Members of the IMF are allocated SDRs. The first allocation occurred in 1970. This additional form of international reserve asset could be looked upon as a form of paper gold (many IMF members looked upon it as a potential replacement for gold in the international monetary system). SDRs can be used to settle indebtedness between countries. A country with a balance of payments deficit can use SDRs for the purpose of purchasing the currencies required.

The timing of the introduction of SDRs was unfortunate. It added to international liquidity at a time when liquidity was overabundant. Since about 1965 the US money supply had risen very rapidly (largely to finance the Vietnam war) and this had led to massive US balance of payments deficits. Those deficits caused a huge flow of US dollars into the foreign exchange reserves of other countries.

The breakdown of the Bretton Woods system

In flooding the international monetary system with dollars the US balance of payments deficits created a situation in which dollars held by countries other than the United States vastly exceeded the United States' own gold and foreign currency reserves. By 1971 US$51 billion were held in countries other than the United States while the US government held only $13.5 billion worth of gold. This meant that the United States was capable of converting only about a quarter of expatriate dollars into gold. This, together with the continuing large US deficits, brought about a collapse of confidence in the US dollar between 1970 and 1971. As foreigners attempted to move their assets out of the dollar, their attempts to sell dollars caused a dollar surplus on international money markets, and this required the US government to deplete its reserves further in order to buy up the surplus and thereby maintain the international value of the dollar. In 1971 there was a rush to have dollars converted into gold by the United States as foreign holders feared a devaluation of the dollar. So great was the pressure that in August 1971 President Nixon announced that the United States would not continue to exchange gold for dollars. That was the last straw. The rush to get out of dollars reached panic proportions.

By the end of the 1960s both the Deutschmark and the yen had become undervalued relative to the US dollar. The Germans and Japanese could either revalue their currencies or maintain the existing par values by intervention. Intervention involved selling their own currencies for dollars so as to keep the prices of the currencies down relative to the US dollar. The Germans and Japanese needed to create more Deutschmarks and yen in order to sell them. When the new Deutschmarks and yen were deposited, by those buying them, in German and Japanese banks the result was an increase in the domestic money supplies of those countries.

In the spring of 1971 the Bundesbank (the German central bank) needed to intervene massively and eventually, having needed to buy US\$1 billion in one hour alone on May 5, suspended intervention. The Deutschmark was allowed to appreciate in value. The suspension of the convertibility of the US dollar into gold in August removed any possibility of the Bundesbank being able to bring the Deutschmark back down to its par value.

An attempt was made to return to a system of fixed exchange rates in December 1971. The new arrangement was known as the Smithsonian Agreement and involved a realignment of currencies, a devaluation of the US dollar in terms of gold (the official price of gold was raised to \$38 per ounce), and a widening of the bands around the par values to $2\frac{1}{4}\%$. However, the scale of intervention required on the part of the Germans and Japanese to maintain the new parities became unacceptable to them and they allowed their currencies to float. So in early 1973 the international monetary system moved to a system of floating exchange rates. The floating rate system has continued since that time.

Floating exchange rates

As dollar holders attempted to sell their dollars for other currencies there was considerable excess demand for currencies other than the dollar. Most of the major trading nations found that they could not flood the international money markets with their own currencies sufficiently to satisfy the demand for them and thereby stem their price increases relative to the US dollar. They had no option but to allow their currencies to rise in value against the dollar. In other words, they abandoned the fixed exchange rates and allowed their currencies to float. The world had suddenly moved from a system of fixed exchange rates to one of floating exchange rates. Meanwhile increased quantities of their own currencies, sold in huge amounts in order to keep down foreign exchange values, found their way back into the national economies of the respective countries as those switching their assets from the dollar invested the newly acquired currencies in the respective countries. Thus many countries experienced massive money supply increases, and the seeds were sown for the worldwide inflation of the early and mid-1970s.

Within the Smithsonian Agreement of December 1971 the major trading nations undertook to return to a regime of fixed exchange rates although at a different set of rates from those that had existed prior to floating. However, the old problems still remained. Furthermore, the rates of inflation being suffered by most countries were higher than they used to be, and there were also greater differences between national rates of inflation. This meant that some countries were being quickly priced out of markets for traded goods and were slipping into severe balance of payments deficits. Some currencies came under downward pressure as holders lost confidence in the maintenance of their value and tried to sell them in order to buy stronger currencies. In June 1972 the British government, after a period of heavy selling of sterling, felt that Britain held insufficient reserves to buy the sterling being sold and thereby maintain its value. The pound was then allowed to float. Sterling was not the only currency to come under pressure. As a result of irresistible pressure, upwards or downwards, other countries returned to floating. By April 1973 the major trading nations had adopted a system of floating exchange rates, a system which remains.

Within a year oil prices had rocketed, so that any lingering hopes of a return to fixed exchange rates were completely destroyed. Oil importing countries, including the United States, suffered massive increases in their import costs. Oil exporters accumulated vast sums of hot money which they were able to switch from one currency to another, putting tremendous pressure on the two currencies, pressure which often could not be withstood even if the countries concerned tried to do so. The emergence of the Organization of Petroleum Exporting Countries (OPEC) must have laid to rest any remaining hopes that countries might be capable of withstanding buying and selling pressure on their currencies.

Despite floating, and largely because of the higher oil prices, the United States experienced further large balance of payments deficits during the 1970s. Largely as a result of the US deficits, worldwide holdings of foreign exchange reserves rose by about 430% between 1969 and 1977 as compared to about 36% between 1964 and 1969. With the US balance of payments deficits persisting reserves of international liquidity continued to accumulate outside the United States.

Third World debt

During the 1970s the eurodollar market provided an easily accessed source of loans for Third World countries. Following the sharp rise in oil prices in 1973–4 oil exporters acquired substantial quantities of dollars which were deposited in international banks. The banks thus had substantial sums to lend and were eager to find borrowers. Third World governments were in need of finance both to fund development programmes and to cover the balance of payments deficits resulting from higher oil prices. Borrowing from official sources such as the IMF tended to have conditions attached, in particular, conditions were often imposed as to the economic policies to be pursued by the borrowing governments. Borrowing eurocurrencies from international banks involved no such conditions and was therefore very attractive.

Heavy borrowing by Third World countries continued through the second half of the 1970s. Both sides to the lending process were encouraged by the tendency for interest rates to be lower than inflation rates so that the rate of debt erosion by inflation exceeded interest payments (the real rate of interest was negative). Events around 1979–80 disrupted this situation. A further sharp increase in oil prices was seen in 1979 which worsened the balance of payments deficits of non-oil exporting developing countries. Their need to borrow correspondingly increased. The other major development was the election of Ronald Reagan as President of the United States of America. The Reagan administration pursued a monetarist economic strategy which resulted in higher dollar interest rates and lower inflation. So real interest rates became positive.

The increased need to borrow together with the emergence of higher rates of interest pushed a number of Third World countries, particularly in Latin America, into a position in which they were unable to service their debts. In some cases borrowers could not even finance the interest costs so they faced increasing debt even if they borrowed nothing more. From the early 1980s debt rescheduling became common place. This involved borrowers and lenders negotiating extended time horizons over which the debts were to be repaid.

The debt rescheduling negotiations provided a new role for the IMF.

A major function of the IMF had been the support of the system of fixed exchange rates by providing member countries with finance when they needed it to support the international values of their currencies. This orientated the IMF primarily towards developed countries. The abandonment of fixed exchange rates in the early 1970s removed this function from the IMF which, in consequence, lost some of its importance.

The need to reschedule Third World debt gave the IMF a new role, and hence increased importance. The IMF became a vital participant in rescheduling negotiations since it, unlike the banks, had the authority to insist on conditions in relation to the economic policies pursued by the debtor governments. Banks often refused to provide further finance in the absence of the imposition of such conditions. This new role gave the IMF an increased orientation towards the less developed countries.

Third World debt has become a traded financial instrument. It is frequently sold at a heavy discount (the price often being less than half the sum owed) reflecting the uncertainty as to eventual repayment. By selling the debt the creditor banks are able to recoup part of the money lent. Despite typically lending as consortiums (thereby reducing exposure to any single debtor), many banks have faced financial problems as a result of the repayment difficulties of the borrowers. Many banks have recorded sharply reduced profits because of the need to make bad debt provision against Third World debt (often this provision amounts to more than half of the sums lent).

The EMS and the ECU

The European Monetary System (EMS) dates from 1979. It represents an attempt by a group of European countries to establish a fixed exchange rate regime in a region. Its membership comprises most of the members of the European Communities. It involves a system of bilateral exchange rates with an expectation that central banks would intervene to ensure that actual rates do not deviate by more than $2\frac{1}{4}\%$ from these central rates. Member countries in the early years of membership sometimes opt for a wider band of 6% deviation from the central rates. A number of member countries envisage the fixed exchange rate system leading to the replacement of the existing national currencies by a common European currency (the ECU).

The main purpose of creating a zone of fixed exchange rates is to enhance trade between the members of the European Communities. When currency values can fluctuate exporters, importers and international

11

investors suffer increased uncertainty as to the size of cash flows when measured in terms of their domestic currencies. For example an importer invoiced in a foreign currency would be faced with higher payments in terms of the home currency in the event of the foreign currency rising in value against the domestic currency. Conversely a company receiving profits from a foreign subsidary would lose in the event of the foreign currency, in which the profits arise, falling relative to the home currency. Variability of exchange rates imparts uncertainty to international trade and investment and hence tends to reduce the extent to which they occur.

The exchange rate mechanism of the European Monetary System does not, however, involve immutably fixed exchange rates. Currency realignments are possible, and have taken place on a number of occasions. The avoidance of such currency realignments requires coordination of economic policy, particularly in relation to inflation. A country with an inflation rate in excess of the Community average would tend to develop a balance of payments deficit and thereby suffer downward pressure on the international value of its currency.

The European Currency Unit (ECU) already exists as a standard of value. It comprises sums of money in each member country currency, with weightings based on the economic importance of the country concerned (at the time of writing the Deutschmark was the largest constituent, at 30.1% of the total, whilst the Greek drachma and Portuguese escudo were the lowest at 0.8% each). The ECU is already an important currency in the eurobond market.

Eurobonds have developed in the wake of the eurocurrency markets. They are bonds whose currency of issue is not the currency of the country in which the issue is made. They provide one means of raising foreign currency. For example, a British company may borrow US dollars by selling dollar-denominated bonds in London. As an alternative to obtaining foreign currency in this way the borrower could issue bonds in the country which is the source of the currency. A non-US borrower can raise dollars by selling bonds in the United States. These are known as Yankee bonds. Yen-denominated bonds sold in Japan by borrowers outside Japan are known as Samurai bonds. Other examples include Bulldog bonds (raising British pounds) and Matador bonds (raising Spanish pesetas). Raising single currencies in this way is suitable if the need is simply for that specific currency. If the need is for a range of currencies, for which some of the borrowed money will be exchanged, there is an exposure to exchange rate risk. A rise in the value of the borrowed currency could raise the value of liabilities relative to assets.

Further reading

When the need is for a range of currencies it would be useful, from the point of view of avoiding exchange rate risk, to borrow a basket of currencies. So selling ECU-denominated bonds, which effectively raises a combination of currencies, may be attractive from the perspective of reducing exposure to the risk of exchange rate movements.

Further reading

J. Orlin Grabbe, *International Financial Markets* (Elsevier, 1986).
Paul Hallwood and Ronald MacDonald, *International Money* (Blackwell, 1986).
Daniel R. Kane, *Principles of International Finance* (Croom Helm, 1988).

2

The foreign exchange markets

The foreign exchange markets trade currencies for both spot and forward delivery. They do not have a specific location and take place primarily by means of telecommunications both within and between countries. There is a number of major financial centres in which the markets are particularly active – New York, London, Tokyo, Frankfurt, Singapore, Hong Kong and Bahrain among others. Much of the market involves trades between banks, whether acting as agents for customers or on their own behalf. Central banks (such as the Federal Reserve, Bank of Tokyo, Bundesbank, Bank of England, etc.) tend to be particularly active participants in the foreign exchange markets, often acting in concert with each other. This intervention by central banks can cause situations in which currency dealers can make trading profits based on technical analysis (the currency markets are possibly the only financial markets that demonstrate sufficient market inefficiency for such trading profits to be made).

Exchange rates are determined by demand and supply. The purchases and sales of currencies stem partly from the need to finance trade in goods and services, although this accounts for only a small percentage of the total (typically much less than 5%). A very substantial proportion is for the finance of investment, in particular, the temporary investment in short-term money market instruments such as bank deposits, that might be regarded as speculation on currency movements (buying and investing the currencies that are expected to appreciate in value). A third source of demand or supply arises from the participation of central banks, a participation that would emanate from a desire to influence the direction, extent or speed of exchange rate movements.

Although short-term speculative movements account for the bulk of currency deals the more fundamental factors of trade in goods and services, long-term investment and government policy are crucial to

14

Foreign exchange markets

currency price movements. Not only do these more fundamental factors have a direct impact but they are in large part the basis for the speculative flows.

Example 2.1

Determination of exchange rates

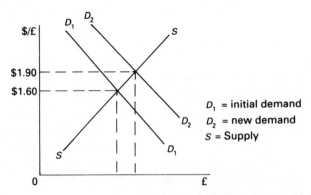

Figure 2.1 Demand and supply determine the international price of the pound

Factors that influence demand and supply
1. The balance of payments on current account, i.e. exports and imports of goods and services.
2. The balance of payaments on capital account, i.e. investment flows into and out of the United Kingdom.
3. Central bank (e.g. Bank of England) intervention.

Figure 2.1 shows the determination of the price of sterling, in terms of the US dollar, by the interaction of demand and supply. The demand for sterling can come from foreign residents paying for UK exports, from foreign residents wishing to invest in the UK, or from the Bank of England (or other central banks) buying sterling in order to support its value. Figure 2.1 illustrates a case in which, as a result of an increase in demand from one or more of these sources, the demand curve for sterling shifts to the right and raises the US dollar value of the pound.

The supply of sterling can arise from UK importers selling pounds in order to obtain the currency required to pay for the imports. It can stem from UK investors wishing to acquire foreign currency in order to invest abroad. Alternatively, one or more central banks may be selling sterling

15

Foreign exchange markets

in order to depress its value. Rightward or leftward shifts (reflecting increased or decreased supply) of the supply curve would generate declines or rises in the price of sterling, respectively.

Example 2.2

The influence of trade in goods and services on the exchange rate

Exports generate a demand by residents of other countries for the sterling required to pay for the UK exports.

Imports generate a demand by UK residents for the foreign currencies needed to pay for imports. Sterling is supplied in payment for the foreign currencies.

An excess of exports over imports implies that the demand for sterling exceeds its supply and vice versa for a deficit.

A current account surplus causes excess demand for sterling and hence an appreciation.

A current account deficit causes an excess supply of sterling and hence a depreciation.

A major cause of surpluses and deficits in the balance of payments on current account is the difference between the UK inflation rate and inflation rates abroad.

Purchasing power parity

Purchasing power parity is a theory of exchange rate behaviour that is useful for explaining long-term currency movements. However, the long term may be as much as five years and purchasing power parity is of little help in explaining short-term changes, particularly day-to-day currency price movements. Despite its shortcomings, purchasing power parity is an important concept. There are two forms of the purchasing power parity theory, the absolute and the relative. The absolute form states that tradable goods should sell at the same price in all countries when adjustments are made for exchange rates and transport costs. If there are differences then arbitrage should take place involving purchasing in the low price countries and selling in the high price countries. Such arbitrage would affect both the prices of the goods concerned and also the prices of the currencies, since the arbitrage trade would involve currency transactions. General misalignments resulting from disequilibrium exchange rates would generate so much arbitrage-based currency trading (buying the currency in which goods are cheap and selling the

16

currency in which they are expensive) that currency prices would be moved towards the values consistent with the absolute form of purchasing power parity. The evidence is not supportive of the absolute form of purchasing power parity but is consistent with the relative form (in the long run).

The relative form of the purchasing power parity hypothesis states that exchange rates will move so as to offset differences between domestic inflation rates. A country experiencing a relatively high inflation rate will tend to experience balance of payments deficits as its goods and services become uncompetitive in international markets. The deficit would put downward pressure on the international value of its currency. Conversely, a country whose inflation rate is low in comparison with that of other countries would find that its exports gain in price competitiveness whilst its imports rise in price relative to domestic production. Its exports would rise and its imports fall. The resulting balance of payments surplus would tend to cause an upward movement in the foreign exchange value of its currency. So the relative form of purchasing power parity predicts that exchange rates will move so as to offset differences between national inflation rates (see Figure 2.2).

Thus, observations of relative rates of inflation, or of the underlying causes such as differences in rates of money supply growth, can be used to ascertain the direction of movement of exchange rates. However, this approach is not suitable for short-run forecasts of exchange rates. Rates can differ from those implied by purchasing power parity for several years and at any one time the actual rates are strongly influenced by

If the UK inflation rate is 4% p.a. higher than the German inflation rate, then purchasing power parity predicts a 4% p.a. fall in sterling against the Deutschmark.

UK has higher inflation

↓

Loss in international competitiveness

↓

Balance of payments deficits

↓

Depreciation

Figure 2.2 Purchasing power parity: exchange rate movements reflect differences in inflation rates

Foreign exchange markets

Table 2.1 Average absolute percentage deviations from purchasing power parity based upon effective exchange rates

	1957–66	1957–72	1957–76
United States	1.2	1.7	3.8
United Kingdom	0.5	3.1	3.8
France	2.5	3.0	3.0
West Germany	1.3	2.1	2.7
Italy	1.2	2.3	5.8
Switzerland	0.7	1.4	5.8
Japan	1.9	2.2	3.8

Source: H. Genberg, Purchasing power parity under fixed and flexible exchange rates, Journal of International Economics (1978) Vol. 8, pp. 246–76.

short-run factors. Not surprisingly, the proportion of exchange rate variability explained by purchasing power parity is greater when there are large differences between countries in the extent to which prices change between two points in time. So the usefulness of the theory is greater when inflation rates differ substantially and when longer time periods are considered, since longer time periods would be associated with larger price-level movements.

Numerous studies, the earliest being soon after the First World War, have tested the relative version of purchasing power parity. On the whole, the studies have shown that over long periods exchange rate variations are well explained by price-level changes.

Exchange rates fluctuate around the rates suggested by purchasing power parity. At any time a currency is likely to be overvalued (relative to the rate implied by purchasing power parity) against some currencies and undervalued against others. Table 2.1 shows some calculations of the average absolute percentage deviations from purchasing power parity based upon effective exchange rates (rates that show a currency's value against a weighted basket of currencies).

Variability around the rate implied by purchasing power parity appears to have increased over time. The switch from fixed to floating exchange rates and the substantial increase in oil prices are two factors occurring in the early 1970s that would help to explain the increased variability.

The movement towards purchasing power parity may occur through exchange rate adjustments, price-level changes, or both, and can take a long time. Studies have suggested that the full adjustment to purchasing power parity can take more than five years, although most of the adjustment is typically achieved within two years.

18

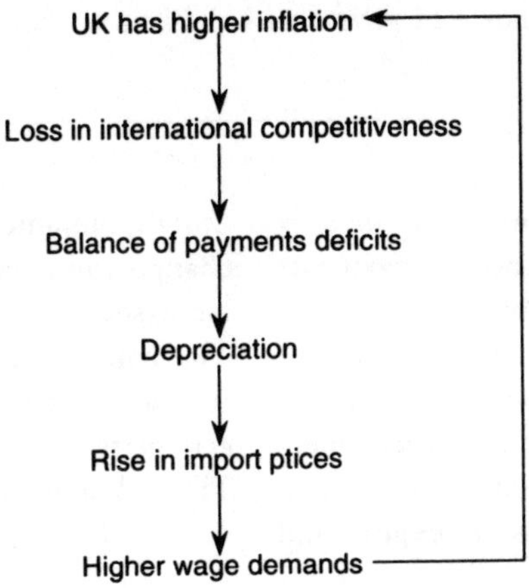

Purchasing power parity

UK has higher inflation ←

↓

Loss in international competitiveness

↓

Balance of payments deficits

↓

Depreciation

↓

Rise in import ptices

↓

Higher wage demands ────

Figure 2.3 There is a danger of a vicious circle where inflation exists

So currency prices should change so as to offset inflation rate differentials. A high inflation rate leads to devaluation of the domestic currency. However, devaluation of the domestic currency causes a rise in import prices. Such a rise in import prices can fuel domestic inflation further, especially if it stimulates increases in the level of wage settlements. This vicious circle is shown in Figure 2.3.

In the short-to-medium term (perhaps for as much as a year following the initial devaluation), there is a strong possibility that a devaluation would weaken the balance of payments and thereby cause an excessive exchange rate adjustment. This can arise from the J curve effect. Trade volumes take time to respond to price changes. Existing orders and contracts will determine trade flows for the first few months. Quantities traded will change only when new orders and contracts are made. However, the price changes are immediate. A country whose currency devalues will face higher import prices from the time of the devaluation. So initially the prices of imported goods rise in domestic currency terms, whilst export and import volumes are unchanged. In the period immediately following the devaluation, expenditure on imports rises with no offsetting increase in export revenues. The initial effect of the devaluation on the balance of payments is to increase the deficit. This worsening of the balance of payments would put further downward pressure on the international value of the domestic currency. So in the short term the depreciation of the currency may be greater than is required for the

19

restoration of balance of payments equilibrium. There is exchange rate overshooting.

Example 2.3

The rise in import prices directly worsens the balance of payments on current account	Initially volumes show insufficient change, but over time the response increases
The changes in the volumes of imports and exports need to be sufficient to offset this direct effect	The balance of payments on current account gets worse before it gets better
Trade volumes take time to respond to changes in export and import prices	This is known as the *J* curve effect

---

Quotation of exchange rates

There are two ways of quoting exchange rates, the direct and the indirect. Most countries use the direct method which involves stating the number of units of domestic currency per one unit of foreign currency. For example, the Deutschmark–US dollar rate might be quoted in Germany as

$$\$1 = DM1.4890–1.4900$$

The indirect method of quotation takes the form of stating the number of units of foreign currency per unit of domestic currency. This method is used in the United Kingdom and the Republic of Ireland. The United States uses the indirect method for all currencies except the British pound, the Irish punt and the ECU, for which the direct method is used. The indirect method produces quotes such as

$$£1 = \$1.9390–1.9400$$

These two examples of exchange rate quotations illustrate two other features of currency price quotation. The first is that exchange rates are often quoted to four places of decimals: the fourth place of decimals is referred to as a point or pip. The second feature is that two prices are always quoted. There is the price at which the customers could buy from a bank, known as the offer or ask price. The other is the price at which the customer could sell to the bank, known as the bid price. The offer price is always greater than the bid price, that is, the bank sells at a higher price than that at which it buys. The difference between these two prices is known as the bid–offer spread or bid–ask spread. In both of the examples of quotations above, the bid–offer spread is ten points. Buying Deutschmarks from a bank would realize DM1.4890 per dollar (the smaller number of Deutschmarks), while selling Deutschmarks to the bank would require DM1.4900 per dollar received (the larger number of Deutchmarks has to be given).

In the interbank market currencies are normally bought and sold against the US dollar. So, for example, buying Swiss francs with Deutschmarks involves buying US dollars with Deutschmarks and then buying Swiss francs with US dollars. Deutschmarks are sold to a bank at the bid price and the dollars received are used to buy Swiss francs at their offer price. The exchange rate between Deutschmarks and Swiss francs obtained by this process is known as a cross-currency exchange rate. Since two bid–offer spreads are involved in the transaction (DM/$ and $/SFr), the Deutschmark/Swiss franc bid–offer spread, which is the difference between the cross-currency rates for Deutschmarks to Swiss francs and for Swiss francs to Deutschmarks, will be proportionately larger than the bid–offer spread of each of the two currencies against the US dollar.

Example 2.4

Cross-currency rates
£1 = $1.9495–1.9505
$1 = DM1.4995–1.5005
£→DM
Sell £ for $1.9495
sell $ for DM1.4995
£1 = 1.9495 × 1.4995 = DM2.9233

DM→£
Buy $ for DM1.5005
buy £ for $1.9505
£1 = 1.9505 × 1.5005 = DM2.9267
£1 = DM2.9233–2.9267
£1 = DM2.92$\frac{1}{4}$–2.92$\frac{3}{4}$

The forward foreign exchange market

A forward purchase is an agreement to buy foreign currency on a specified future date at a rate of exchange determined in the present. Likewise a forward sale. This technique removes uncertainty as to how much future payables or receivables are worth in terms of domestic currency.

A particular type of money market transaction that involves a forward operation is the swap. A swap consists of the spot purchase of a currency

Table 2.2 Pound spot-forward against the pound

Dec. 7	Day's spread	Close	One month	% p.a.	Three months	% p.a.
US	1.9430–1.9520	1.9510–1.9520	0.95–0.93cpm	5.78	2.53–2.50pm	5.16
Canada	2.2570–2.2665	2.2620–2.2630	0.38–0.32cpm	1.86	0.68–0.59pm	1.12
Netherlands	3.2500–3.2625	3.2500–3.2600	$1\frac{3}{4}$–$1\frac{1}{4}$cpm	4.84	$3\frac{1}{2}$–$3\frac{1}{4}$pm	4.15
Belgium	59.50–59.95	59.85–59.95	24–18cpm	4.21	58–48pm	3.54
Denmark	11.0950–11.1400	11.1050–11.1150	$3\frac{3}{4}$–$3\frac{3}{8}$orepm	3.85	$8\frac{5}{8}$–$7\frac{3}{4}$ pm	2.95
Ireland	1.0780–1.0920	1.0815–1.0825	0.30–0.25cpm	3.05	0.75–0.63pm	2.55
Germany	2.8790–2.8900	2.8850–2.8900	$1\frac{1}{4}$–1pfpm	4.68	3–$2\frac{3}{4}$pm	3.98
Portugal	253.25–255.15	254.00–255.00	1–22dis	–0.54	97–158dis	–2.00
Spain	183.80–184.95	183.85–184.15	2–10cais	–0.39	36–49dis	–0.92
Italy	2171.75–2177.50	2174.50–2175.50	4–3lirepm	1.93	8–6pm	1.29
Norway	11.2950–11.3375	11.3125–11.3225	$3\frac{5}{8}$–$2\frac{1}{4}$orepm	3.11	$5\frac{5}{8}$–$5\frac{1}{8}$pm	1.90
France	9.7750–9.8050	9.7925–9.8025	$3\frac{3}{8}$–$3\frac{1}{8}$pm	3.98	$7\frac{7}{8}$–$7\frac{1}{4}$pm	3.14
Sweden	10.8475–10.8925	10.8700–10.8800	par–$\frac{1}{4}$oredis	–0.14	$2\frac{1}{8}$–$3\frac{1}{4}$dis	–1.03
Japan	255.25–256.75	255.70–255.80	$1\frac{1}{4}$–$1\frac{1}{8}$ypm	5.57	$3\frac{3}{8}$–$3\frac{1}{8}$pm	5.18
Austria	20.25–20.30	20.26–20.29	$8\frac{1}{8}$–$7\frac{3}{8}$gropm	4.59	$22\frac{5}{8}$–$20\frac{1}{4}$pm	4.23
Switzerland	2.4575–2.4675	2.4575–2.4675	$1\frac{1}{8}$–1cpm	5.18	$2\frac{1}{8}$–$2\frac{1}{4}$pm	4.57
Ecu	1.4025–1.4120	1.4100–1.4110	0.46–0.42cpm	3.74	1.04–0.99pm	2.88

Commercial rates taken towards the end of London trading. Six-month forward dollar 4.54–4.49cpm. 12 month 7.86–7.76cpm.

Premiums and discounts

and the simultaneous forward sale of the same currency (or spot sale and forward purchase). When a forward transaction is not part of a swap operation it is referred to as an 'outright' deal. Outright forward transactions can be for the purposes of either hedging or speculating. The facility of knowing the rate of exchange for a transaction in advance eliminates the risk of adverse movements of the exchange rate, and hence provides a means of hedging foreign exchange risk. Speculators may undertake forward positions in the expectation that the spot rate that will prevail on the day the forward contract matures will differ from the forward rate obtained. If a speculator expects the spot rate on a particular day to be lower than the forward rate relating to that day, a sale forward will be made in the anticipation that, when that day arrives, it will be possible to buy at a cheaper price than the contracted sale price. Thus a profit is made in the process of meeting the forward commitment. Likewise a speculator expecting the spot rate to be higher than the forward rate will buy forward in the anticipation of being able to sell the currency bought at a higher price on the spot market.

Premiums and discounts

If the forward rate for a currency exceeds the spot rate, that currency is said to be at a premium. For example, if the spot rate of sterling in terms of US dollars is £1 = $1.40, whilst the six-month forward rate is £1 = $1.45 then sterling is said to be at a premium against the dollar. Conversely, if the forward rate is less than the spot rate the currency is said to be at a discount. With a spot exchange rate of £1 = $1.40, a forward rate of £1 = $1.35 means that sterling is at a discount against the US dollar (correspondingly the dollar is at a premium against sterling).

Table 2.2 shows how forward rates against sterling are reported in *The Financial Times*. The letters 'pm' indicate that the currency is at a premium against sterling and 'dis' indicates a discount. The forward rates are obtained by subtracting the premium from, or adding the discount to, the quoted price of sterling. For example, the spot price for sterling at the close of business is quoted as US$1.9510–1.9520 (sterling can be sold for $1.9510 per £1 and bought for $1.9520), and the dollar is at a three-month premium of 2.53–2.50 cents. This implies a forward rate of $1.9257–1.9270.

Table 2.3 shows how forward rates against the US dollar are quoted in *The Financial Times*. On the date concerned (7 December, 1990) every currency stood at a discount to the US dollar. In most cases the discount

Table 2.3 Dollar spot-forward against the dollar

Dec 7	Day's spread	Close	One month	% p.a.	Three months	% p.a.
UK†	1.9430–1.9520	1.9510–1.9520	0.95–0.93cpm	5.78	2.53–2.50pm	5.16
Ireland†	1.7935–1.8055	1.8045–1.8055	0.30–0.25cpm	1.83	1.20–1.10pm	2.55
Canada	1.1575–1.1630	1.1585–1.1595	0.38–0.40cdis	−4.04	1.09–1.13dis	−3.83
Netherlands	1.6650–1.6775	1.6680–1.6690	0.16–0.19cdis	−1.26	0.54–0.58dis	−1.34
Belgium	30.60–30.75	30.65–30.75	2–4cdis	−1.17	9–15dis	−1.56
Denmark	5.6900–5.7250	5.6900–5.6950	0.90–1.10oredis	−2.11	3.20–3.80dis	−2.46
Germany	1.4755–1.4880	1.4790–1.4800	0.12–0.14pfdis	−1.05	0.47–0.50dis	−1.31
Portugal	130.55–131.15	130.60–130.70	62–72cdis	−6.15	230–260dis	−7.50
Spain	94.40–95.05	94.50–94.60	47–52cdis	−6.28	145–155dis	−6.35
Italy	1112.50–1121.50	1114.25–1114.75	3.50–4.00liredis	−4.04	11.20–12.20dis	−4.20
Norway	5.7900–5.8300	5.7975–5.8025	1.35–1.70oredis	−3.16	4.80–5.40dis	−3.52
France	5.0100–5.0450	5.0175–5.0225	0.68–0.73cdis	−1.69	2.66–2.76dis	−2.16
Sweden	5.5665–5.5940	5.5700–5.5750	2.60–2.90oredis	−5.92	8.60–9.20dis	−6.39
Japan	130.40–132.15	131.05–131.15	0.01–0.03ydis	−0.18	0.06–0.09dis	−0.23
Austria	10.4175–10.4480	10.4175–10.4225	0.50–1.10gdis	−0.92	2.30–3.60dis	−1.13
Switzerland	1.2585–1.2710	1.2620–1.2630	0.07–0.10cdis	−0.81	0.24–0.29dis	−0.84
Ecu	1.3800–1.3900	1.3805–1.3815	0.25–0.23pm	2.09	0.85–0.79pm	2.38

Commercial rates taken towards the end of London trading. †UK, Ireland and ECU are quoted in US currency. Forward premiums and discounts apply to the US dollar and not to the individual currency.

Premiums and discounts

Table 2.4

	yen/$		yen/$
Spot	131.05–131.15	Spot spread	0.10
One month forward discount	0.01–0.03	Spread on discount	0.02
One month forward rate	131.06–131.18	One month forward spread	0.12

Table 2.5

	$/ECU		$/ECU
Spot	1.3805–1.3815	Spot spread	0.0010
One month forward premium	0.0025–0.0023	Spread on premium	0.0002
One month forward rate	1.3780–1.3792	One month forward spread	0.0012

of the currency against the US dollar is signified by 'dis'. In the cases of the British pound, Irish punt and the ECU it is signified by 'pm' because these three currencies use the direct form of quotation against the US dollar (dollars per unit of foreign currency), whereas the other currency quotes are based on the indirect form (number of units of foreign currency to the US dollar). The rule of thumb is that the adjustment for the premium or discount produces a forward bid–offer spread that is greater than the spot bid–offer spread. Take, for example, the yen against the dollar (see Table 2.4).

The discount or premium should be added or subtracted with the result that the forward spread is greater than the spot spread. As another example, consider a direct form of quote, that of the ECU against the dollar (see Table 2.5).

In both cases adjustment for the premium or discount widens the bid–offer spread. In the first case, the dollar is worth more yen forward than spot, so the yen is at a discount against the US dollar. In the second case, the ECU is worth fewer dollars forward than spot, so the US dollar is at a premium against the ECU.

The premiums and discounts are also reported in terms of per cent per annum. In Table 2.2 the dollar premium is quoted as 5.16% p.a. This percentage is ascertained from the following formula:

$$\frac{\text{premium} \times 365 \times 100}{\text{spot rate} \times \text{number of days to maturity}}$$

This formula can be more readily understood by rewriting it as:

$$\text{percentage} = \frac{\text{premium}}{\text{spot rate}} \times \frac{365}{\text{number of days to maturity}} \times 100$$

25

The first component, premium/spot rate, expresses the premium as a proportion of the spot rate. The second component, 365/number of days to maturity, annualizes the figure. It alters the first ratio to produce the number that would be found for the twelve-month premium if the twelve-month forward premium was proportional to the three-month (or whatever) premium. So in the case of three-month forwards this adjustment would multiply the first ratio by four, whilst in the case of one-month forwards the multiplication would be by about twelve. Finally, the resulting figure is multiplied by 100 in order to convert the decimal into a percentage.

Example 2.5

Spot £1 = $1.9510–1.9520
3-month forward premium = 2.53–2.50 cents
3-month forward rate is £1 = $1.9257–1.9270

Rate of premium (% p.a.)
For seller of sterling

$$\frac{0.0253}{1.9510} \times 4 = 0.0519 \ (5.19\% \ \text{p.a.})$$

For buyer of sterling

$$\frac{0.0250}{1.9520} \times 4 = 0.0512 \ (5.12\% \ \text{p.a.})$$

Mid-price quote

$$\frac{0.025\,15}{1.9515} \times 4 = 0.0516 \ (5.16\% \ \text{p.a.})$$

The bid–offer spread (the difference between the buying and selling prices) is always larger for forward foreign exchange than for spot. From Table 2.2 it can be seen that, in the case of the US dollar, the spot spread is 0.1 cent ($1.9510–$1.9520) whilst the three-month forward spread is 0.13 cent. It is thus possible to see whether there is a premium or a discount even in the absence of a direct indication (in the case of the Reuters board there is no indication such as 'pm' and 'dis'). The quoted numbers should be added to, or subtracted from, the spot numbers according to whichever increases the bid–offer spread. So in the case of

Determination of forward rates

the three-month forward rate against the US dollar the spread is increased by subtracting 2.53–2.50 from the spot prices. It follows that the US dollar is at a premium against the pound (the pound is at a discount against the dollar). In the case of the Spanish peseta the numbers for the three-month forward rate are 36–49. The bid–offer spread is increased by adding these to the spot rates to yield 184.21–184.64. The peseta is thus at a discount against sterling.

Example 2.6

Spot £1 = $1.9495–1.9505
Three-month forward premium = 2.50–2.47 cents
Three-month forward rate is £1 = $1.9245–1.9258
Spot bid–offer spread = $0.0010
Forward bid–offer spread = $0.0013
Forward spread > spot spread
Forward spread = spot spread + premium spread

Determination of forward rates

To build up the picture of how forward exchange rates are determined it is useful to begin with considering how a bank might deal with a customer's request to buy or sell foreign currency forward. For example, a customer wishes to sell US$1 million for sterling six months forward. To avoid exchange risk the bank could sell dollars at the time that the forward deal is agreed. The dollars might be obtained by borrowing them at the current eurodollar rate and the sterling obtained would be invested. Suppose that eurodollar six-month interest rates are 15% p.a. and eurosterling six-month rates are 10% p.a. The position of the bank immediately after the forward deal is agreed is:

10 March
   Borrows $930,232 ($1,000,000/1.075) at 15% p.a.
   Buys   £620,155 (930,232/1.5) at the spot exchange rate of
           £1 = $1.50
   Deposits   £620,155 at 10%

10 September
   Receives $1,000,000 from customer
   Repays $930,232 capital plus $69,768 interest (totalling $1,000,000)

Foreign exchange markets

Receives   £620,155 capital plus £31,008 interest (totalling £651,163)

Pays customer   £651,163

On 10 March the bank agrees to pay the customer £651,163 in exchange for $1,000,000 on 10 September. The forward exchange rate is thus

$$\$1,000,000/£651,163 = \$1.5357/£1$$

(Note that for this example, figures have been rounded to the nearest whole pound or nearest whole dollar). Although it is possible, rather than probable, that a bank would follow this procedure, its possibility means that should the forward rate differ from £1 = $1.5357, the bank could profitably use this technique. Competition between profit-maximizing banks in the pursuit of customers would then move the forward rate towards the one calculated above.

The forward exchange rate calculated above can alternatively be calculated by means of the equation:

$$\frac{R_F - R_D}{1 + R_D} = \frac{F - S}{S}$$

where R_F is the eurocurrency interest rate on the foreign currency, R_D is the eurocurrency interest rate on the domestic currency, F is the forward (or futures) exchange rate, and S is the spot exchange rate. The condition depicted by this equation is known as interest rate parity. Using the figures from the example above (and treating sterling as the domestic currency), gives:

$$\frac{0.075 - 0.05}{1.05} = \frac{F - 1.5}{1.5}$$

$$F = 1.5357$$

A point to be noted is that since six-month forwards are being dealt with, the annual interest rates need to be converted to six-month rates by dividing by 2 (e.g. 15% p.a. equals 7.5% over six months, which in decimal form is 0.075). Secondly, the exchange rate needs to be quoted using the indirect method (units of foreign currency per unit of domestic currency), so if, in the above case, the US dollar was the domestic currency:

$$\frac{0.05 - 0.075}{1.075} = \frac{F - 0.6667}{0.6667}$$

$$F = 0.6512 \ (1/1.5357)$$

28

Determination of forward rates

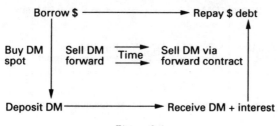

Figure 2.4

The interest rate parity relationship can alternatively be looked upon in terms of arbitrage possibilities, in particular, covered interest arbitrage. Interest returns should be the same on all currencies (specifically eurocurrencies) when account is taken of forward premiums and discounts. Thus, there is no significant difference in terms of return between investing in a dollar deposit (in the case above at 15% p.a.) on one hand and buying sterling spot, whilst selling it forward and investing that sterling between purchase and sale on the other hand. The forward premium on sterling offsets the interest differential between dollar and sterling deposits. This is the interest rate parity relationship.

The 'rule of thumb' is that if interest rates on foreign currency deposits are higher than those on domestic currency deposits then the domestic currency will be at a premium against foreign currency, whereas if the domestic currency interest rates are the higher, then the domestic currency will be at a discount. The premium or discount compensates for the interest rate differential between deposits in the two currencies (note that the relevant rates are those on eurocurrency deposits).

The interest rate parity relationship may be maintained by covered interest arbitrage. Taking the example of the Deutschmark against the US dollar, the arbitrage may take one of the following forms.

1. Borrow dollars, buy spot Deutschmarks with the borrowed dollars; deposit the Deutschmarks purchased, sell those Deutschmarks plus interest forward; use the dollar receipts to repay the dollar borrowing. This is illustrated by Figure 2.4.
2. Borrow Deutschmarks, sell those Deutschmarks in the spot market for US dollars; deposit the dollars, buy forward Deutschmarks against the original dollars plus anticipated interest; use the Deutschmark receipts to repay the Deutschmark borrowing. This is illustrated by Figure 2.5.

29

Foreign exchange markets

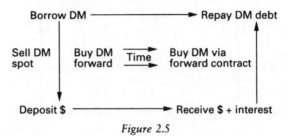

Figure 2.5

It is to be emphasized that all values are known at the outset: dollar interest rates, Deutschmark interest rates, spot exchange rates, forward exchange rates. Since all relevant values are known no risk attaches to the arbitrage transactions. So, if interest rate parity fails to hold one of the two arbitrage processes illustrated will yield a riskless profit.

The arbitrage process will tend to restore interest rate parity if it is deviated from, and hence the interest rate parity relationship is maintained by the mechanism of covered interest arbitrage. This arbitrage involves making profits from divergences between the interest rate differential, on the one hand, and the premium/discount expressed as a percentage change from the spot exchange rate on the other.

Suppose that the sterling short-term interest rate is 10% p.a., whilst the corresponding dollar rate is 8% p.a. The dollar stands at a premium against sterling and this premium implies an appreciation of the dollar at a rate of 2% p.a. Suppose further that this interest rate parity relationship is disturbed by an increase in the dollar interest rate to 9% p.a. An opportunity for arbitrage profits emerges. A bank in the UK could borrow sterling at 10% p.a., exchange it for dollars, deposit those dollars at 9% p.a. and simultaneously sell the principal plus interest forward. Inclusive of the 2% p.a. guaranteed appreciation of the dollar, the dollar deposit yields 11% p.a. in terms of sterling. There is a net gain of 1% p.a., and there is no risk involved. This arbitrage is illustrated by Figure 2.6. (Note that for the purposes of exposition there has been some rounding to the nearest whole number.)

The process of taking advantage of the arbitrage opportunities tends to restore interest rate parity. In particular, the spot purchase of dollars tends to raise the spot price of dollars, and the forward sale of dollars tends to depress the forward price. The rising spot price and falling forward price reduces the dollar's premium. The premium will decline so long as the arbitrage is pursued and the arbitrage will be pursued so long as the premium exceeds the interest rate differential. In Figure 2.6 there is scope for arbitrage profits so long as the dollar's premium

30

Determination of forward rates

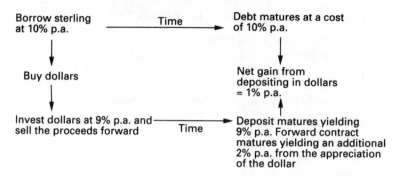

Figure 2.6

against sterling exceeds 1% p.a. (In addition, borrowing sterling and lending dollars tends to raise sterling interest rates relative to dollar rates so that a widening interest rate differential may contribute to the restoration of interest rate parity.)

Exercise 2.1

Question
The interest rate parity relationship can be expressed as

$$\frac{R_\$ - R_£}{1 + R_£} = \frac{F - S}{S}$$

where $R_\$ = $ US dollar interest rate, $R_£ = $ sterling interest rate, $F = $ forward price of sterling and $S = $ spot price of sterling. If twelve month rates are

$$£ \quad 13\tfrac{11}{16} - 13\tfrac{9}{16}$$

$$\$ \quad 8\tfrac{5}{16} - 8\tfrac{3}{16}$$

and spot £1 = $1.9260–1.9270,

(a) between what forward prices (for twelve-month forwards) would there be no opportunity for arbitrage profits?
(b) If the interest rates above were three-month rates what would be the theoretical prices of forward contracts maturing in three months?

Answer

(a) Borrow $, buy spot £, deposit £, sell £ forward.

$$\frac{0.083\,125 - 0.135\,625}{1.135\,625} = \frac{F - 1.9270}{1.9270}$$

$$F = \$1.8379/£1$$

31

Foreign exchange markets

Borrow £, sell spot £, deposit \$, buy £ forward.

$$\frac{0.081\,875 - 0.136\,875}{1.136\,875} = \frac{F - 1.9260}{1.9260}$$

$F = \$1.8328/£1$

There would be no scope for arbitrage profits between

£1 = \$1.8328 and £1 = \$1.8379

It must be remembered that money is borrowed at the offer rate (which is the higher rate) deposited at the bid rate (which is the lower rate). Currency is bought at the offer (higher) price and sold at the bid (lower) price.

(b) $$\frac{0.020\,781 - 0.033\,906}{1.033\,906} = \frac{F - 1.9270}{1.9270}$$

$F = \$1.9025/£1$

$$\frac{0.020\,469 - 0.034\,219}{1.034\,219} = \frac{F - 1.9260}{1.9260}$$

$F = \$1.9004/£1$

So the range of theoretical forward prices would be

\$1.9004/£1 to \$1.9025/£1

Cause and effect

Interest rate parity establishes a close relationship between the spot exchange rate and the forward exchange rate. The question arises, however, as to whether the spot rate is determined by market forces and the forward rate follows it or whether the forward rate takes the lead and the spot rate follows. There are advocates of both views. There are two good reasons for supposing that the forward rate determines the spot rate. Firstly, changes in the underlying economic and political circumstances seem likely to lead to a greater volume of forward deals than spot deals. Bodies deciding to hedge previously unhedged positions because of the changes would do so in the forward market. Speculators seeking to profit from their anticipations of exchange rate movements are likely to do so using forward rather than spot exchange because of the higher leverage involved in forward positions. (Futures could be used as alternatives to forwards and would behave in a similar way.)

Secondly, there is reason to believe that the forward rate corresponds to the expected rate and is therefore not determined by the spot rate.

Cause and effect

Speculators have expectations about the level of future exchange rates and if forward rates differ from these expectations there is a perceived scope for speculative gains. Furthermore, the pursuit of these speculative gains would tend to move the forward rate towards the expected rate. Suppose, for example, that the three-month forward rate was above the rate that was generally expected. It would be worthwhile to sell forward with a view to honouring the contract by means of buying spot when the contract matures. If the expectation is correct the currency is bought at a lower price than that at which it is sold. Conversely, a forward rate lower than the expected rate would lead speculators to buy forward in anticipation of selling at a higher price when the contract matures. In the former case the forward sales by speculators would depress the forward rate towards the expected rate whereas in the latter case their forward purchases would raise the forward rate towards the expected rate. So there is reason to believe that the forward rate would tend to represent the expected rate. Since the expected rate is unlikely to be mechanistically determined by the spot rate it seems plausible that the line of causation goes from the forward rate to the spot rate.

For example, if sterling looks as though it might weaken because oil prices have fallen, previously unhedged positions might become hedged. Potential hedgers may be prepared to leave positions exposed until the fear of a sterling depreciation emerges. The emergence of such a fear leads to forward sales in order to avert the risk of loss from a considerable depreciation. Traders may also enter the forward market in the antici-pation of making profits. If a trader expects the future spot rate to be below the forward rate he sells forward with a view to meeting the forward contract when it matures by buying spot at a lower price. The total effect is to drive down the forward price of sterling.

An increasing forward discount (or decreasing premium) for sterling would render sterling deposits less attractive relative to deposits in other currencies. The rate of depreciation of sterling would exceed the interest differential in favour of sterling. Arbitrageurs would sell sterling spot in order to switch their investments from sterling to other currencies. This puts downward pressure on spot sterling which declines in value thereby maintaining interest rate parity. Thus the forward sales of sterling bring about matching depreciations of forward and spot sterling leaving the premium/discount unaffected (unless there has been some impact on the interest rate differential).

Finally, in this context, it is interesting to note that futures rates are frequently used as a source of information by operators in the spot

Foreign exchange markets

market. This use of futures rates suggests that they are seen as being determined independently of spot rates. Since forward rates are unlikely to diverge significantly from futures rates it follows that forward rates are also seen as being determined independently of spot exchange rates.

Having considered the basic concepts underlying currency forwards, techniques are now examined for dealing with problems arising in the use of forwards – such as extending forwards, dealing with uncertain cash flow dates, hedging when no direct forwards exist between two currencies, ascertaining forward rates for irregular dates, and hedging the contingent risks that accompany tenders.

EXTENDING A FORWARD CONTRACT

It may be that the date on which a cash flow is due is postponed. A hedger with a forward contract might then need to extend the contract. The extension is likely to involve the first contract being settled by means of an opposite contract and a new contract being agreed. (This is often referred to as a forward swap or a forward/forward swap.)

For example, on 1 May a hedger buys sterling three months forward against US dollars at a forward rate of £1 = $1.50. By 1 July it is clear that the exchange of currencies will be delayed by a month. The hedger needs a forward contract for 1 September. The 1 August contract is settled and a 1 September contract agreed. The settlement of the first contract will involve a payment or receipt if the 1 August forward rate has changed since 1 May. Consider the following rates:

1 May	Three-month forward rate	£1 = $1.50
1 July	One-month forward rate	£1 = $1.48
	Two-month forward rate	£1 = $1.47

The contract taken out on 1 May to buy sterling at £1 = $1.50 on 1 August is settled on 1 July by taking out a contract to sell the same amount of sterling at £1 = $1.48 on 1 August. There is a loss of 2 cents per £1.

On 1 July a contract to buy sterling at £1 = $1.47 on 1 September is taken out. Taking the 2 cents per £1 loss into account the effective forward price of sterling is £1 = $1.49.

An alternative approach would be to take the difference between the August and September rates on 1 July and apply it to the original forward rate. In the preceding example, sterling is at a 1 cent discount between 1 August and 1 September. Extending a forward contract from 1 August

Cause and effect

to 1 September could take the form of applying the August to September discount to the original forward rate. The forward rate thereby obtained would be $1.50 − $0.01 = $1.49. (Although this is the same as the effective forward rate obtained by means of the previous technique the two rates may not turn out to be precisely the same.)

OPTION DATE FORWARD CONTRACTS

Normally, forward contracts relate to a single future maturity date. However, such fixed date contracts may not be ideal for a customer who is uncertain as to when he will receive, or need to provide, foreign currency. In such a case, it is possible to obtain a forward option contract whose maturity date lies within a range of dates, the customer having the right to choose the specific date.

The customer pays a price for this degree of flexibility since the forward rate will be the least favorable fixed date contract rate for the period. Suppose, for example, that the two-month forward rate for sterling against the US dollar is £1 = $1.40, whilst the three-month forward rate is £1 = $1.39. A customer wanting to buy sterling sometime between two and three months would pay the higher price, which is $1.40. The bank providing the contract assumes that the chosen maturity date will be the least favorable from the point of view of the bank. Likewise someone selling sterling forward would receive the rate of £1–$1.39. The bank assumes that the chosen maturity date will fall at the end of the period.

The bank determines the forward rates in this way in order to avoid losses. The consequence is that the customer may be quoted a rate that is very unfavorable compared with fixed date forward contracts. Because an option date forward is likely to entail an unfavorable rate a hedger might prefer taking out a fixed date forward and then entering a forward swap when the date on which currency is to be exchanged becomes certain.

CURRENCY HOLD ACCOUNTS

A less expensive means of adding flexibility to forward exchange contracts is the use of currency hold accounts. These are suitable for companies faced with continuous flows of business in a foreign currency. They are bank accounts in the relevant foreign currencies. If the holder of a forward contract to buy a currency finds that the currency is needed later than expected, the currency purchased under the forward contract is deposited

35

in the hold account until it is required. Conversely, if the currency is needed before the maturity date of the forward contract the company goes into overdraft in order to meet its foreign currency payment and subsequently pays off the overdraft with the currency purchased when the forward contract matures.

OVERLAPPING OPTION DATE FORWARDS

Option date forwards normally allow the customer to spread out the currency transactions rather than requiring the total purchase or sale to be conducted on one day. This is particularly convenient for a company anticipating a stream of payments or receipts, as opposed to occasional isolated payments/receipts.

The tendency to be quoted the most disadvantageous fixed date price available over the relevant period leads customers to use the shortest possible option date period, since this may eliminate the most unfavorable rates. Shortening the option period increases the uncertainty as to whether the relevant payments/receipts will fall within that period. These conflicting influences on the choice of option period can be reconciled by means of overlapping option date forwards.

This procedure involves covering part of the currency flow with short period options and the remainder with longer period options. For example, currency receipts may be expected in each of three future months but only two-thirds of the anticipated monthly receipts is expected with certainty to accrue during the relevant month. Two-thirds of the total receipts would be covered by one-month options and the remainder might be covered by an option date forward extending over the full three months. As currency is received during a month the forward sale facility specific to that month is used first, and when it is used up the remaining receipts in that month are sold using the three-month option facility.

FORWARD CROSS RATES

It may be the case that the forward market between two currencies is illiquid, or even non-existent. In such a situation, forward cover might be generated by using two separate forward transactions using a third currency. For example, a Spanish importer may wish to buy Canadian dollars forward. If the forward market between Spanish pesetas and Canadian dollars was inadequate, the Spanish importer could choose to buy US dollars forward, against Spanish pesetas, and simultaneously sell

Cause and effect

the US dollars forward, against Canadian dollars. The forward rate effectively obtained for Canadian dollars against Spanish pesetas is a cross rate.

Suppose that the market rates for three-month forwards are as follows:

US$/peseta spot	160.00	160.10
3-month premium	0.20	0.27
		160.37
US$/Canadian $ Spot	1.4000	1.4010
3-month premium	0.0015	0.0020
	1.4015	

The importer buys US dollars with pesetas paying 160.37 pesetas per US dollar, and then buys Canadian dollars with the US dollars received, obtaining 1.4015 Canadian dollars per US dollar. The importer pays 160.37 pesetas and receives 1.4015 Canadian dollars, thus paying: 160.37/1.4015 = 114.43 pesetas per Canadian dollar. This is the three-month forward buying cross price of Canadian dollars against Spanish pesetas.

Foreign exchange transactions that use a vehicle currency, which is most often the US dollar, involve suffering the bid–offer spread twice. In the example above, the US dollar is purchased for the higher of two prices and sold for the lower of two prices.

The premium or discount between the two currencies can be ascertained by reference to the spot cross rate. In the present example, the spot cross rate is 160.10/1.4000 = 114.36 pesetas per Canadian dollar. The peseta is at a discount against the Canadian dollar (of 0.24% p.a.).

INDIRECT FORWARDS

If the currency for which the company wishes to obtain cover is part of a currency bloc, or has a fairly stable relationship with a major currency, there is scope for indirect cover. For example, if an American firm wanted to cover foreign exchange risk arising from being invoiced in Danish kroner and found that forward cover against the kroner for the relevant period was not available, it could look to the Deutschmark instead. Denmark and Germany are both participants in the exchange rate mechanism of the European Monetary System. The resulting stability between the kroner and the Deutschmark means that the American firm can operate by means of cover against the Deutschmark. If the American

37

firm needs to pay in kroner at a future date it can buy Deutschmarks forward and then, upon receipt of the Deutschmarks, sell them spot for kroner.

There are standard contract periods for forward transactions. These standard periods are one, two, three, six and twelve months (forwards can, however, be obtained for more distant dates). A forward deal with a 'broken date' is one whose period falls between two standard periods, for example, nine months.

The exchange rate for a broken date forward contract is obtained by interpolation. The difference between the rates for the two closest standard period dates is divided by the number of intervening days. The result is multiplied by the number of days between the broken date and the later standard period date. The figure obtained is subtracted from, or added to, the forward rate relevant to the later date to obtain the forward rate of the broken date.

Suppose that the three-month forward rate for sterling against the US dollar is $1.40 whilst the six-month forward rate is $1.37. The four-month forward rate is calculated as follows:

$$\text{three-month rate} - \text{six-month rate} = \$1.40 - \$1.37 = \$0.03$$
$$\$0.03 \times \tfrac{60}{90} = \$0.02$$

(assuming that 90 days elapse between the two standard maturity dates and 60 days separate the four-month broken date from the six-month standard date). The 2 cents is added to the six-month rate in order to obtain the four-month rate:

$$\$1.37 + \$0.02 = \$1.39$$

A bank agreeing to a forward purchase or sale by a customer will want to lay off the risk that arises. For example, if a customer takes out a contract to buy US dollars against sterling on a future date, the bank acquires a risk that the dollar will have risen above the agreed forward price by that date. The bank risks having to sell dollars at a price lower than that which it buys, so the bank will want to hedge.

One way in which the bank could reduce its risk would be to buy the dollars spot and invest them pending maturity of the forward contract.

Cause and effect

There are other approaches that the bank may choose. It may buy forward itself from another bank or it could use financial futures. To the extent that customers have offsetting requirements, the need to use external hedging instruments is reduced. If there were customers wishing to sell dollars forward on the same maturity date that the forward buyer seeks, the bank would find that risks offset each other. To the extent that forward deals offset each other, the bank will be able to transfer currencies between customers without being exposed itself. The bank's exposure would be limited to the discrepancy between forward sales and forward purchases. It is this net exposure that needs to be hedged.

TENDERING

Tendering for contracts poses a particular problem from the point of view of covering foreign exchange risk. The exporter faces an exchange rate risk from the date that the tender is decided upon. However, with some types of hedging the exporter would be exposed to risk in the event of the tender proving to be unsuccessful. For example, if the hoped-for currency receipts were sold on the forward market and the tender then turned out to be unsuccessful, the tendering company would be committed to a forward sale with no corresponding long position in that currency. It would be exposed to the risk of an increase in the price of the currency. Such an appreciation could produce a situation in which, in order to meet the forward sale, the company must purchase (spot or forward) at a higher price. So companies that tender are interested in hedging techniques that do not leave them exposed in the event of the tender being unsuccessful.

Tender to Contract schemes offer forward contracts that become operative only in the event of the tender being successful. The unsuccessful tenderer is not left with an uncovered forward position, as would be the case with normal forward currency transactions. The cover is also cheaper than that provided by options. Option premiums are charged in the light of the potential gain to the option holder in the event of the spot price of the currency being sold turning out to be lower than the selling price guaranteed by the contract, and the absence of any possibility of loss arising through the spot price being higher than the agreed exercise price (since the option holder retains the right to sell spot). Under the Tender to Contract scheme, if the tender is successful the exporter has no choice but to sell at the agreed forward price. So there is not the possibility, offered by options, of ignoring the hedging contract and selling spot if the spot price turns out to be higher than the agreed exercise price. The hedger must endure the loss of selling at the agreed forward price when the spot price of the currency is higher, and correspondingly the bank benefits from the gains involved. Hence the fee to be paid for cover under the Tender to Contract scheme would be less than the costs involved when using options. (Another factor raising the cost of using an option relative to Tender to Contract is the possibility of exercising the option at a profit when the tender is unsuccessful and the spot price of the currency is less than the selling price guaranteed by the option.)

By forfaiting, an exporter is able to transfer an exchange rate risk (and credit risk) on to a bank. The process involves the exporter receiving a cash payment from the forfaiter, who in turn obtains the claim on the payment for the exports. Bills of exchange and promissory notes are the types of trade debt most commonly forfaited, although receipts on open account may be forfaited. The money received by the exporter is equal to the anticipated payment for the exports minus a discount. The discount rate is based upon the eurocurrency interest rate for the currency involved (there may be a further discount based on the credit risk).

The exchange of foreign currency for the home currency takes place when the goods are delivered, or when the trade paper is received, and so there is no need to hedge foreign exchange risk from that date. Nevertheless, there is hedging implicit in the rate of discount. This is because of the interest rate parity relationship. If the currency of invoice is at a discount in the forward exchange market its eurocurrency interest rate will be correspondingly at a relatively high level. So the rate of interest at which receivables are discounted is relatively high when the currency of invoice is at a discount against the home currency (vice versa for a premium). So for the period between delivery of the goods and receipt of money in payment from the importer, hedging exchange rate risk by forfaiting is equivalent in cost to hedging by means of forward selling. (The discount rate on the foreign currency receivables equals the domestic currency interest rate plus the forward discount of the foreign currency, or minus the forward premium.)

Forward rates as forecasts

There is reason to believe that the forward rate corresponds to the expected rate. Speculators have expectations about the levels of future exchange rates and if forward rates differ from these expectations there is a perceived scope for speculative gains. Furthermore, the pursuit of these speculative gains would tend to move the forward rate towards the expected rate.

For example, suppose the three-month forward rate was above the rate that was generally expected. It would be worthwhile to sell forward exchange with a view to honouring the contract by means of buying spot when the contract matures. If the expectation is correct, the currency is bought at a lower price than that at which it is sold. Conversely, a forward rate lower than the expected rate would lead speculators to buy forward in anticipation of selling at a higher price when the contract matures. In the former case, the forward sales by speculators would depress the forward rate towards the expected rate whereas in the latter case their forward purchases would raise the forward rate towards the expected rate.

The forward rate may not precisely reflect expectations of the future rate because no forecast is held with certainty. The speculator's forecast may turn out to be wrong and as a result a loss might be incurred. The expected profit must be sufficient to at least compensate for this risk. If the forward rate does not differ from the expected rate by enough to offer an expected profit more than sufficient to offset the risk, the forward purchase or sale would not be undertaken. In addition to compensating for the risk the profit must also cover the transactions costs (commissions and bid–offer spreads). So there will be a range of forward prices, around the expected price, that do not offer sufficient profit to entice speculators. The greater the perceived risk, and the higher the transactions costs, the wider this range will be. In highly volatile, and hence very risky, market conditions the extent of the range may be considerable. Under such circumstances the value of forward, or futures, prices as market forecasts is much reduced.

There is therefore reason to believe that the forward rate would tend to approximate to the expected rate. Forward and futures prices are frequently used as sources of price information by operators in the spot market. This use of forward and futures prices suggests that the expected rate is reflected in forward and futures rates.

It appears that forward rates are generally as likely to overestimate as to underestimate future currency prices. The absence of any significant tendency towards overestimation or underestimation suggests that forward rates are unbiased predictors of future rates. An unbiased predictor has no net tendency towards either underestimation or overestimation, but may none the less be typically inaccurate. Perfect accuracy of any forecast is impossible since not all circumstances that will affect an exchange rate can be foreseen. The most that can be hoped for is that the market for forward foreign exchange is efficient. An efficient market is one that utilizes all available information in the determination of prices and in which the price adjustments are made quickly. If the markets for forward currency are not efficient there may be scope for obtaining better forecasts from other sources, for example, when other sources utilize all the available information.

Forecasting services

If forward exchange rates do not fully utilize all the available information then there is scope for professional exchange rate forecasters to provide more accurate forecasts by making more effective use of the available information. Also, if a forward exchange rate differed from the expected spot rate because of a risk premium or transaction costs, there would be scope for professional forecasters to provide a better prediction than that obtained by observing the forward exchange rate. In the view of many, including the present author, any suggestion that professional forecasts tend to be more accurate than forward rates must be regarded as not proven. Indeed, if it were the case that professional forecasts were better predictors of rates because they made better use of the available information, it is to be expected that the process of obtaining speculative profit would pull forward rates into line with the forecasts thereby eliminating the superiority of the forecasts.

Case study

Using forwards to restructure debts
1. A company has purchased a mainframe computer from an American firm for $6,000,000, payable in four annual instalments. The first instalment is payable immediately. The US company allows credit at 6% p.a. The purchaser, whose revenues are in sterling, is at risk from an appreciation of the US dollar against sterling. The purchaser shops around for forward contracts and finds that the UK subsidiary of an American bank is prepared to offer, one, two and three-year forward contracts at £1 = $1.47, £1 = $1.44 and £1 = $1.41, respectively. The spot rate is £1 = $1.50. The purchaser agrees to buy forward dollars as follows:

1 year hence $1,590,000 for £1,081,632
2 years hence $1,685,400 for £1,170,416
3 years hence $1,786,524 for £1,267,038

The future sterling cash flows are thus predetermined and exchange rate risk is eliminated. Effectively, the 6% p.a. dollar liability is converted to a sterling liability of about 8% p.a.

2. A company wishes to borrow 10 million Finnish markka for two years but can only borrow on a six-month floating rate basis. Forward contracts can be used to create a liability on a fixed rate basis.

The company borrows 2 million eurodollars for two years at 6% p.a. The spot exchange rate is $1 = 5 markka and the two-year forward rate is $1 = 5.10 markka. The company buys 10 million markka spot and agrees to a forward sale of markka as follows:

2 years hence   11,460,720 markka for $2,247,200

To repay the 2 million eurodollar loan, US$2,247,200 is required. The company has guaranteed that 11,460,720 markka will be required at the end of the two years. This sum is equivalent to a fixed annual rate of about 7% on the initial 10 million markka.

Case study

Calculating forward exchange rates
If twelve-month interest rates are

$$£ \quad 13\tfrac{11}{16} - 13\tfrac{9}{16}$$

$$\$ \quad 8\tfrac{5}{16} - 8\tfrac{3}{16}$$

and spot £1 = $1.9260–1.9270

(a) If a UK company requested a six-month forward purchase of US dollars from a bank what forward exchange rate might be expected?

(b) If the company requested a six-month forward sale of US dollars to the bank, what forward rate might be obtained?

(a) Action by bank

Day 1
Borrow £ (e.g. 1,000,000) at $13\tfrac{11}{16}$%
Buy $1,926,000 and deposit at $8\tfrac{3}{16}$%

Foreign exchange markets

Day 183

£ debt = £1,000,000 × 1.068 4375 = £1,068,437.5

$ asset = $1,926,000 × 1.040 9375 = $2,004,845.6

For six-month forward on Day 1 the bank would accept £1,068,437.5 (to repay £ debt) for $2,004,845.6.

Forward exchange rate £1 = $1.8764

(b) *Action by bank*

Day 1

Borrow $ (e.g. 1,000,000) at $8\frac{5}{16}\%$

Buy £518,941.36 (1,000,000/1.927) and deposit at $13\frac{9}{16}\%$

Day 183

$ debt = $1,000,000 × 1.041 5625 = $1,041,562.5

£ asset = £518,941.36 × 1.067 8125 = £554,132.07

For six-month forward on Day 1 the bank would accept $1,041,562.5 (to repay $ debt) for £554,132.07.

Forward exchange rate £1 = $1.8796

Further reading

Christian Davies and Michael Feeny, *Exchange Rate Forecasting* (Woodhead-Faulkner, 1989).

Daniel R. Kane, *Principles of International Finance* (Croom Helm, 1988).

Maurice D. Levi, *International Finance* (McGraw-Hill, 1990).

3

~

Money markets and interest rates

The short-term money markets

TREASURY BILLS

Treasury bills are instruments issued on behalf of governments for the purposes of raising short-term finance and implementing monetary policy. They have been particularly important in the United States and the United Kingdom. They are pure discount instruments, that is, they pay no interest and the return to the holder arises entirely from capital appreciation. Upon maturity they are redeemed for their nominal values. Buyers purchase them at a discount to the nominal values. Treasury bills are marketable so that the original purchaser of a bill is able to sell it prior to its maturity date. The selling price will reflect the nominal price and current interest rates. It is likely that each successive holder of a bill will participate in the profit from that bill.

Consider a UK Treasury bill redeemable for £100,000 with a 91 day maturity and issued at a discount of 12% p.a. The initial purchase price would be £97,000. The buyer could hold the bill to maturity and receive the £100,000 (note that this 12% p.a. rate of discount is equivalent to the rate of interest of £3,000/£97,000 multiplied by four, which is $12\frac{3}{8}$% p.a.). Alternatively the original buyer might sell the bill before maturity. A sale occurring after 30 days, in a context of unchanged interest rates, would involve a sale price of £97,000 plus (30/91) × £3,000, which amounts to £97,989. (Note that in the United States three months is treated as 90 days rather than 91 days so that the sale price would have been $97,000 plus (30/90) × $3,000, i.e. $98,000.)

The example just cited assumed unchanged interest rates. Discount rates would tend to move in line with interest rates on debts of similar maturity. If at the end of the 30 days the discount rate had risen to 15% p.a., the price at which the bill changed hands would have been

£100,000 minus (61/91) × (0.15/4) × £100,000 = £97,486.26 ($97,500 in the United States). The increase in the discount rate from 12% p.a. to 15% p.a. approximately halves the profit to the original buyer of the bill (equivalent to an interest return being offset by a capital loss).

Treasury bills can be regarded as being free of default risk, and their short periods to redemption provide them with a high degree of capital certainty (the scope for capital losses is limited). These features help to render treasury bills highly liquid, as does the active secondary market. Treasury bills are therefore popular as short-term assets and their rate of return is often treated as a riskless rate which can be used as a benchmark for rates of return on other short-term financial instruments.

BILLS OF EXCHANGE (COMMERCIAL BILLS)

Bills of Exchange are means of providing trade credit. The seller of the goods or services addresses an order in writing to the buyer. The issuer of the bill (the drawer) makes out the bill with the consent of the counterparty (the drawee) who accepts it by signing it. Bills of Exchange are negotiable in the money market so that the drawer can obtain funds immediately by selling the bill. The bill would be sold at a discount to the sum receivable from the drawee at maturity. That discount would provide the return to the buyer of the bill.

Bank bills are Bills of Exchange accepted by banks. A bank accepting a bill guarantees that the holder will receive the payment due upon maturity of the bill. Bank bills thus bear little or no default risk. A Bill of Exchange accepted (guaranteed) by a party other than a bank is known as a trade bill. A fine trade bill, whilst not having been accepted, is relatively secure because both the drawer and drawee are reputable parties. Bills of Exchange with low (or zero) default risk can be sold in the secondary market at relatively low rates of discount (and hence high prices) and might be regarded as close substitutes for treasury bills.

COMMERCIAL PAPER

Commercial paper is another means of raising short-term finance. Unlike Bills of Exchange, commercial paper issues are not related to specific transactions. They are a means of borrowing on a short-term basis that constitutes an alternative to borrowing from banks. In the United Kingdom, maturities may not exceed one year and issuing companies must have net assets of at least £50 million and be listed on the stock exchange. In France, issues may be made only by companies based in France and all issues up to two years' maturity must be backed by credit lines equal to 75% of their values (in France commercial paper is known as *billets de trésorerie*). In most countries, commercial paper is rated by rating agencies. However, in Sweden, which has one of the largest commercial paper markets outside North America, rating is not undertaken and back-up credit is not legally required.

INTERBANK DEPOSITS AND CERTIFICATES OF DEPOSIT

The interbank market involves banks lending to and borrowing from one another. It is a wholesale money market with individual deposits being large in size. It is important to the financial intermediation function of the banking system as a whole. A bank may receive a substantial deposit of a particular maturity without being aware of potential borrowers seeking that maturity. However, another bank may have such a potential borrower. The first bank would on-lend to the second bank. The banks may contact each other directly or could be brought together by a money broker. Money brokers specialize in bringing borrowers and lenders together and, in doing so, seeking out the most advantageous rates of interest for their clients. A sum of money may be on-lent through a chain of banks between the initial (non-bank) depositor and the ultimate (non-bank) borrower.

Interbank transactions can take the form of either normal deposit taking or the issue of Certificates of Deposit (CDs). Non-bank participants such as corporates and fund managers may also buy CDs in preference to simply depositing money.

A CD is issued by a bank in return for a deposit of money for a fixed term. Certificates of Deposit have a secondary market, in other words the holder of a CD is able to sell it to a third party in order to realize money before the maturity date of the CD. The issuing bank has money for a known term whilst the depositor has an asset that can be immediately liquidated by means of a sale. The bank can borrow fixed-term money at finer rates than otherwise whilst depositors can enjoy improved rates on liquid deposits (normally money at call would yield a lower interest rate than a fixed term deposit, CDs permit fixed-term borrowing by banks to constitute money at call for depositors and both benefit from the disappearance of the interest rate differential).

Certificates of Deposit are (except in the United States) bearer instruments. The buyer is not registered. The rights accruing to the certificate are enjoyed by the body in possession of it and the issuing bank will simply pay the sum due at maturity to whoever presents the certificate.

Unlike other instruments traded in the short-term money markets CDs tend to be interest bearing rather than providing a yield by means of being initially sold at a discount. However, since the rate of interest is fixed at the time of issue any subsequent changes in market rates would be reflected in the emergence of discounts or premiums. Also, since the seller of a CD would not receive the interest payment (which would usually be payable at maturity), a price would be expected that reflects the accrued interest, in other words the price of the CD would be enhanced so that the seller receives their share of the interest yield.

Certificates of Deposit are not only issued in national currencies but also in currency baskets, particularly SDRs.

Eurocurrency markets

The markets for treasury bills and Bills of Exchange are often referred to as the traditional money markets whereas the markets for commercial paper, interbank deposits and Certificates of Deposit are known as the parallel money markets.

The parallel money markets operate both in domestic currency and eurocurrencies. The eurocurrency markets involve the instrument used being denominated in a currency that is foreign to the country in which the instrument is created or traded. A US dollar deposit in a London bank would be a eurodollar deposit. A sterling-denominated Certificate of Deposit issued by a Paris bank would be a eurosterling CD. A yen-denominated commercial paper issue sold outside Japan would constitute euroyen commercial paper. Like parallel money market instruments the eurocurrency dimension is global.

The determination of interest rates

Considering this matter from a domestic perspective the question subdivides into two: What determines world interest rates? What causes domestic rates to deviate from world rates?

The principle of interest rate parity suggests that domestic rates should bear a close relationship to rates elsewhere. According to this principle, interest rates around the world would tend to be equal when account is taken of expectations of exchange rate movements (as reflected by forward exchange rate premiums and discounts). Arbitrage, the process whereby money moves between financial centres in search of the highest return, brings interest rates into line. If sterling rates exceed dollar rates, money flows from dollar deposits to sterling and this lowers the return on sterling deposits relative to dollar returns. The qualification that account is taken of expected exchange rate movements is an important one.

If sterling is expected to depreciate against the dollar, sterling interest rates must exceed dollar rates by a margin sufficient to compensate for the anticipated exchange rate loss from holding sterling. For example, if sterling is expected to depreciate at 4% p.a. against the US dollar the rate of interest on sterling deposits must be 4% p.a. higher to compensate. In this way, expected returns on different currencies are equalized. To be precise, the relevant currency appreciation or depreciation is the one reflected by the premium or discount on forward foreign exchange contracts.

Example 3.1

Interest rate parity
The difference between sterling interest rates and interest rates on other currencies

is equal to

The expected rate of appreciation/depreciation of sterling against those other currencies.

For example: If sterling is expected to fall by 3% p.a. against the US dollar, interest rates on sterling would be 3% p.a. higher than those on US dollars in order to compensate for the expected depreciation.

An interest rate can be looked upon as a price payable for loanable funds. Potential borrowers provide the demand for loans, and lenders the supply. The interaction of demand and supply determines the price (the interest rate). If borrowers outweigh lenders, interest rates will be bid up, conversely an excess supply of loanable funds leads to a fall in rates.

Government economic policy is an important factor in the determination of interest rates. An excess of government spending over revenues means that the government must enter the market to compete for loans with private borrowers. The government's demands for funds can add considerably to the pressure on interest rates.

Money markets and interest rates

Example 3.2

Interest rates can be regarded as being determined by the interaction of the demand for, and supply of, loanable funds.

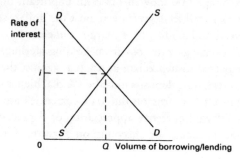

Figure 3.1 Determination of interest rates

The demand for loanable funds, DD, comes from borrowers and the supply of loanable funds, SS, comes from lenders.

The market for loanable funds is now global. The global demand and supply determine the 'world' interest rate.

The 'world' interest rate might be looked upon as an average of individual countries' interest rates.

Example 3.3

An increase in the demand for funds to finance investment, consumer spending or government budget deficits would shift the demand curve to the right and raise interest rates.

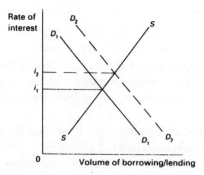

Figure 3.2 The effect of government budget deficits on interest rates

Determination of interest rates

An increase in interest rates from a higher demand for funds from one source, e.g. government budget deficits, would choke off ('crowd out') the demand for other purposes, e.g. investment and consumer spending.

Example 3.4

An increase in the supply of loanable funds would shift the supply curve to the right and lower interest rates.

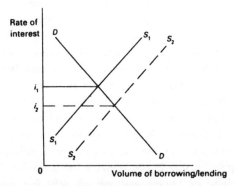

Figure 3.3 The effect of loanable funds on interest rates

An increase in the propensity to save (by individuals and/or firms) would cause a rightward shift of the supply curve.

The expected rate of inflation is one factor affecting the interest rate at which borrowers and lenders will transact. When inflation is expected, potential lenders will seek compensation for the anticipated erosion of the purchasing power of their assets and will correspondingly require higher interest rates. Borrowers, in anticipation of liabilities being eroded by inflation, may be prepared to pay higher rates. Thus the interest rate incorporates compensation for expected inflation.

Example 3.5

Real and nominal interest rates
Inflation erodes the purchasing power of money and hence of assets/ liabilities denominated in money.
This erosion of the value of assets should be subtracted from nominal interest receipts in order to ascertain the real interest rate.

Money markets and interest rates

Likewise the erosion of the value of liabilities should be subtracted from nominal interest payments in order to ascertain the real interest cost.

Real interest rate = Nominal interest rate — Expected rate of inflation

---

Despite the important role of interest rates on currencies other than the domestic currency, specifically domestic factors have an influence on domestic currency interest rates. A particularly important domestic factor is government monetary policy. The influence of domestic factors does not mean that interest rate parity fails to hold. If domestic factors change interest rate differentials between currencies, then spot and forward exchange rates would move so as to maintain interest rate parity.

Government monetary policy is a major domestic factor in interest rate determination. Such policy is executed by a central bank which may be largely independent of other government authorities (as is the Federal Reserve in the United States and the Bundesbank in Germany) or may be subordinated to other government authorities (for example, the Bank of England is subordinate to the UK Treasury). If a central bank wishes to influence interest rates it would normally exert its influence by altering the demand/supply balance in the loanable funds market. This could be achieved by selling or buying government debt instruments such as Treasury bills or bonds. Such buying or selling of debt instruments is often referred to as open market operations, and frequently has its effects via altering the liquidity of the banking system.

If the central bank sells bills or bonds the purchasers make payment by drawing on their bank accounts. This involves a transfer of money to the central bank from the other banks. This may leave the banking system with a cash deficiency. The banks (via discount houses in some banking systems) might then turn to the central bank for loans. The central bank would lend at an interest rate that reflects the new level of rates that it wishes to see. A rise in interest rates is achieved by selling debt in order to reduce banks' liquidity (selling debt constitutes a government demand for loanable funds), whereas a reduction in interest rates is achieved by means of government buying debt (thereby increasing the supply of loanable funds) and hence generating a surplus of bank liquidity.

Example 3.6

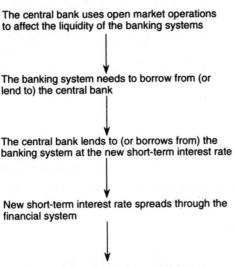

The central bank uses open market operations to affect the liquidity of the banking systems

↓

The banking system needs to borrow from (or lend to) the central bank

↓

The central bank lends to (or borrows from) the banking system at the new short-term interest rate

↓

New short-term interest rate spreads through the financial system

↓

Longer-term interest rates respond if the new short-term interest rate is expected to persist

The liquidity preference approach

Whereas the loanable funds approach sees interest rates as determined by the interaction of the flows of borrowing and lending (demand for and supply of loanable funds), the liquidity preference approach regards interest rates as determined by the relationship between the stock of money and the demand for money. Money would be defined as banknotes and bank deposits. The quantity of money that is desired to be held appears to increase as interest rates fall (possibly because this indicates lower returns on other forms of holding financial assets). The liquidity preference approach suggests that interest rates will be such as to equate the demand for money with the available supply. This is illustrated by Figure 3.4 (which makes the simplifying assumption that the supply of money is unresponsive to the interest rate, the conclusions of the analysis are not affected if this assumption is dropped).

It may be noted that shortly after the stock market crash of October 1987 a number of central banks increased their national money supplies. The reasons can be seen in terms of the liquidity preference theory.

Money markets and interest rates

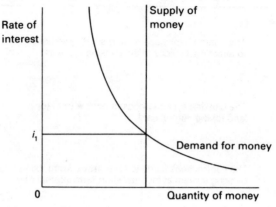

Figure 3.4 The liquidity preference approach to interest rate determination

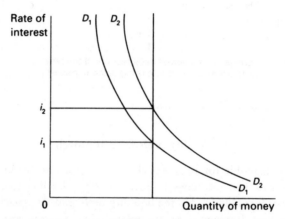

Figure 3.5 The effect of demand for money on interest rates

After the crash many fund managers sold stock with a view to holding money instead. This constituted a substantial rise in the demand for money. Such an increase in the demand for money would have tended to raise interest rates, as illustrated by Figure 3.5.

A further rise in interest rates at that time could have precipitated another stock market crash. In order to avert such an eventuality, central banks in a number of countries increased their national money supplies. As a result the supply of money rose in line with the demand and a sharp increase in interest rates was avoided.

Forward/forward interest rates

Forward/forward interest rates are rates for periods commencing at points of time in the future and are implied by current rates for differing maturities. For example, the current three-month interest rate and the current six-month interest rate between them imply a rate for a three-month period which runs from a point in time three months from the present until a point in time six months hence.

Borrowing for six months and depositing for three months effectively creates a three-month borrowing deferred for three months (the three-month deposit offsets the first three months of the borrowing). Depositing for six months and borrowing for three creates a three-month deposit deferred for three months (during the first three months the asset and liability offset each other). The current three- and six-month interest rates imply rates for the deferred period, these implied rates are the forward/forward interest rates. Consider the following data.

Spot three-month $\qquad 8\frac{15}{16} - 9\frac{1}{16}$

Spot six-month $\qquad 9\frac{15}{16} - 10\frac{1}{16}$

The forward/forward three month rate for a period commencing three months from the present is the rate that would yield the same return as the spot six-month rate, when compounded with the current three-month rate. Using mid-rates from the above figures:

$$(1.0225)(1 + x) = (1.05)$$

0.0225 is the decimal rate for three months based on 9% p.a. and 0.05 is the decimal rate for six months based on 10% p.a. The rate x is the forward/forward rate and is given by:

$$x = (1.05/1.0225) - 1$$
$$= 0.0269$$

which is 2.69% over three months and hence 10.76% per annum (multiplying 2.69% by four).

It may seem strange that the implied rate is not 11% p.a. since at first sight it might seem that the six-month rate would equal the average of the two three-month rates. Since the first three-month rate is 9% p.a., then to average 10% p.a. the second should be 11% p.a. The forward/forward rate is less than 11% because there is compounding of the second three-month rate on the first whereas the six-month rate involves no compounding. The effect of the compounding is that the second three-month rate is less than 11% p.a.

It is interesting to note that if the spot three and six-month rates are the same, then the forward/forward rate will be lower than both of them. If both the three and six-month rates were 10% p.a. then:

$$(1.025)(1 + x) = (1.05)$$
$$x = (1.05/1.025) - 1$$
$$= 0.0244$$

i.e. 2.44% per quarter or 9.76% per annum. Again this is because the two successive three-month rates benefit from compounding whereas the six-month rate does not.

Thus far the analysis has been based on mid-rates. It is necessary to examine the effects of using the bid and offer rates. Different foward/forward rates emerge according to whether the deferred rate is for a borrowing or a deposit. Returning to the first example and considering a deferred borrowing, the six-month rate would be $10\frac{1}{16}$% p.a. whilst the three-month rate would be $8\frac{15}{16}$% p.a. (the six-month borrowing would be at an offer rate whereas the three-month deposit would be at a bid rate).

$$(1.02234)(1 + x) = (1.050\,31)$$
$$x = (1.050\,31/1.022\,34) - 1$$
$$= 0.0274$$

(2.74% over three months, which is 10.96% per annum). The corresponding deferred deposit would involve depositing for six months at $9\frac{15}{16}$% p.a. whilst borrowing for three months at $9\frac{1}{16}$% p.a.

$$(1.022\,66)(1 + x) = (1.049\,69)$$
$$x = (1.049\,69/1.022\,66) - 1$$
$$= 0.0264$$

(2.64% over three months, which is 10.56% per annum). So the forward/forward borrowing (i.e. offer) rate is 10.96% p.a. whereas the corresponding forward/forward deposit (i.e. bid) rate is 10.56% p.a. The spread is 0.4% p.a. which approximates to $\frac{3}{8}$% p.a. It is to be noted that the forward/forward bid–offer spread is considerably larger than the spot market spread.

The forward/forward rates are used as a basis for the calculation of fair prices for three-month interest rate futures and for forward rate agreements (FRAs).

Forward rate agreements

Forward rate agreements (FRAs)

Forward rate agreements (FRAs), sometimes referred to as future rate agreements, provide a technique for locking in future short-term interest rates.

HEDGING WITH FRAS

Risk is reduced by entering a notional agreement to lend or borrow in the future at a rate of interest determined in the present. A set of bid–offer spreads is published showing rates of interest for different future time periods, for example the published spreads for sterling might indicate a bid–offer spread of 10.750 00–10.625 00 for sterling lent for a two-month period starting one month from the present, and 10.875 00–10.750 00 for a three-month period commencing nine months from the present. The customer and the bank agree that compensation will pass between them in respect of any deviation of interest rates, on the date that the loan was due to be made, from the rates published at the time of the agreement.

For example, a corporation has a floating rate loan of £1 million and would like to be certain as to what rate of interest it will be charged on the loan for the three-month period commencing three months from the present. It might ascertain from the published bid–offer spreads that for sterling three-month loans, taken out three months from the present, the spread is 10.625 00–10.500 00. The corporation could attempt to guarantee what its interest rate will be by entering an FRA, thereby notionally committing itself to borrow £1 million at 10.625% in three months' time. A settlement interest rate is used for calculation of the compensation payment to pass between the counterparties. Suppose that the spread for this rate stood at 11.625 00–11.500 00 when the contract period was reached. The 1% p.a. increase in rates would require the bank to pay the customer a sum equivalent to 1% p.a. for three months on a £1 million loan – totalling about £2,500. The money received would compensate the corporation for a rise in the rate of interest on its floating rate loan over the three-month period.

The change in the interest rate payable on a floating rate loan is likely to be equal to, or close to, the change in the settlement interest rate. Had interest rates fallen, the compensation payment would have been made in the opposite direction so that the corporation would have lost on its FRA but gained from the lower rate on its floating rate loan. In either case an interest rate variation on the loan would have been offset

57

by a gain or loss on the FRA. The corporation would have achieved its aim of removing uncertainty as to the interest payable.

The actual compensation is slightly less than £2,500. This gross sum is discounted at the settlement interest rate since the compensation is paid at the beginning of the interest period whereas the higher interest on the floating rate loan is paid at the end of the interest period. The compensation, plus interest obtainable on it during the interest period, would equal £2,500.

The interest rate that the parties attempt to lock in is not necessarily the current rate at the time of entering the FRA. The rate obtained by means of the FRA would reflect the forward/forward interest rate.

Example 3.6

These points may be clarified with the help of a numerical example. The example illustrates the case of a corporate borrower with a floating rate loan of £1 million on which the interest rate is reassessed on a six-monthly basis. The latest reassessment has set the interest rate at 12% p.a. whilst the settlement interest rate is currently 11.000 00–10.875 00. The treasurer wishes to hedge the risk of a rise in interest rates by the date of the next interest rate reassessment. The FRA market is currently quoting 11.500 00–11.375 00 for six months against twelve months (interest rates for six-month loans made six months from the present). The company decides to hedge by buying FRAs, thereby notionally committing itself to borrow £1 million six months hence. By the beginning of the interest period the spread stands at 12.500 00–12.375 00 and the interest on the floating rate loan is $13\frac{1}{2}$% p.a.

Interest rate	*FRA spread*
1 February	
Interest rate for February–July is set at 12% p.a. and LIBOR stands at 11.000 00–10.875 00. The company seeks to hedge against an interest rate increase occurring by 1 August.	Buys FRAs for six-month interest period commencing 1 August. The FRA interest spread is 11.500 00–11.375 00.
1 August.	
Interest rate for August–January is set at $13\frac{1}{2}$% p.a. An extra $1\frac{1}{2}$% must be paid, amounting to £7,500 ($1\frac{1}{2}$% on £1 million for six months).	The FRA spread stands at 12.500 00–12.375 00. Compensation is receivable in respect of 1% on £1 million for six months, amounting to £5,000.

Forward rate agreements

The borrower suffers a loss of £7,500 which is offset by a £5,000 FRA gain. On 1 February the FRA spread was 11.500 00–11.375 00. The FRA gains and losses offset realized deviations from $12\frac{1}{2}\%$ p.a. so that the effective interest payable, net of compensation, is $12\frac{1}{2}\%$ p.a. The corporation has eliminated uncertainty about the future interest rates payable on its floating rate debt.

The removal of uncertainty would be incomplete if the interest rate charged on the loan could change by an extent different from the change in the settlement interest rate. For instance, if the interest on the loan in the example had risen to $13\frac{5}{8}\%$ p.a. then the interest rate increase, net of compensation, would have been $\frac{5}{8}\%$. The borrower would have failed to guarantee a net increase of $\frac{1}{2}\%$. However, changes in borrowing rates are likely to be similar to settlement interest changes so that most of the uncertainty is removed.

CLOSING OUT

An FRA need not be held until maturity, it can be closed out at any time by entering into a second FRA which is opposite to the original one. The success of hedging operations does not depend upon holding FRAs to maturity. To completely close out an FRA position, the second FRA must involve the same principal amount as the first. The interest period would also be the same but the interest rate would probably be different. The published interest rate spread for the relevant future period may have changed between the date of entering into the first FRA and the date of starting the opposing one. Such a difference would lead to a compensation payment. A hedger may originally buy, notionally committing himself to borrow, and subsequently close out by selling, notionally comitting himself to lend. If, for example, the notional obligation to borrow is at a lower interest rate than that at which there is a notional obligation to lend, there is a net gain which is received in the form of a compensation payment. The compensation received upon closing out would offset the higher interest payable on the floating rate loan.

COMPENSATION FORMULA

The payment made upon maturity of an FRA is given by the formula

$$\frac{(Rs - Rf) \times (N/Y) \times A}{1 + Rs(N/Y)}$$

where Rs = settlement interest rate (when the FRA matures); Rf = FRA guaranteed interest rate (when the FRA is agreed); N = period (in days)

On 15 July LIBOR stands

Money markets and interest rates

of borrowing/lending to which the FRA relates; Y = number of days in a year (365 for sterling, 360 for other currencies); and A = sum of money to which the FRA relates.

Case study

Seasonal borrowing

A toy company has a seasonal borrowing requirement for the period July–October for the purpose of financing the stocks required to meet the pre-Christmas sales. On 15 January it uses an FRA to guarantee the interest payable on a £2 million three-month loan to be taken out on 15 July. On 15 January the rate for three-month LIBOR six-months forward is 10% p.a. Anticipating a borrowing at LIBOR + $1\frac{1}{4}$%, the toy company thus locks in an interest rate of $11\frac{1}{4}$% p.a.

On 15 July LIBOR stands at 12% p.a. The company could borrow £2 million at $13\frac{1}{4}$% p.a., which involves a repayment of £2,066, 250 on 15 October. However, the bank providing the FRA compensates for the deviation of LIBOR on 15 July from 10% p.a. The compensation payment is 2% p.a. for three months on £2 million discounted at LIBOR to reflect the fact that the compensation is paid at the beginning of the period, whereas interest is payable at the end of the period. The sum paid by the bank to the toy company on 15 July is £9,786. The company thus borrows £1,990,214 instead of £2,000,000. At $13\frac{1}{4}$% p.a. the sum to be repaid on 15 October is £2,056,682. This is equivalent to paying 11.244% p.a. on £2 million for the three-month period. By using the FRA, the toy company has locked in an interest rate of about $11\frac{1}{4}$% p.a. and has thus avoided the 2% p.a. rise in interest rates.

$$\frac{(0.12-0.1) \times (92/365) \times £2,000,000}{1+0.12(92/365)} = £9,786$$

The bank providing the FRA need not be the bank providing the loan. Indeed the FRA might be provided through a money broker rather than a bank. The cash flows under the FRA are limited to the money value of the deviation of LIBOR from the agreed future interest rate.

The term structure of interest rates

The term structure of interest rates is the relationship between yields on instruments and their maturities. The graphical presentation of the

Term structure of interest rates

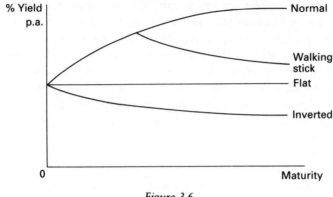

Figure 3.6

structure is known as the yield curve. Figure 3.6 illustrates some possible yield curves.

On the far left of the yield curve the instruments are very short-term deposits that can be withdrawn without notice, or with just a few days' notice. On the far right the instruments have very distant maturities and would include items such as twenty-five-year government bonds.

The most common yield curve has been the one labelled 'normal' in Figure 3.6. It depicts the typical pattern, which is that of relatively low yields at the short end of the spectrum and higher rates at the long end but with a tendency to flatten out at the long end with the effect that, for example, the yield on twenty-five-year government bonds is only marginally higher than that on ten-year government bonds.

Explanations of the term structure themselves follow a spectrum from the pure expectations theory, to expectations adjusted for risk, to the notion of preferred habitat, and the idea of market segmentation at the other extreme. These approaches can be distinguished by their views as to substitutability between instruments of different maturities. The pure expectations theory regards different maturities as perfect substitutes for each other. The perceived substitutability declines through the spectrum of theories until the market segmentation approach with its perspective of zero substitutability between bands of maturities.

PURE EXPECTATIONS

According to this view long-term interest rates are averages of expected short-term rates. For example, the five-year rate would be seen as an

61

average of the current six-month rate, the six-month rate anticipated for six months from the present, the six-month rate expected to prevail one year hence, and so on. In other words, the annualized rate of return on instruments with a five-year maturity would equal the average annualized rate of return on the next ten six-month instruments. An investor is seen as having the choice of buying a five-year instrument or depositing money for six months and then redepositing the proceeds for a further six months and so on. The pure expectations approach takes the view that investors would be indifferent as to which of these alternative investment routes is taken. If rates of return differ between these alternatives investors will move from the one yielding less to that yielding more, and this process will bring the yields into line with each other (for example, if five-year bonds produced the higher yield investors would seek to buy more and this additional demand would pull up the bond prices and thereby lower their yields).

This approach encompasses all maturities. One-month rates are averages of seven-day rates, three-month rates are averages of actual and expected one-month rates, one-year rates are based on successive three-month rates, yields on five-year bonds are derived from expected one-year yields, and a twenty-year bond is seen as equivalent to four successive five-year bonds. The pure expectations approach regards instruments as perfect substitutes for one another throughout the spectrum of maturities. If a twenty-five-year government bond provides a slightly higher rate of return than the expected yield from a succession of seven-day deposits, then investors would switch from seven-day deposits to twenty-five-year bonds and in so doing alter demand and supply conditions for the instruments so as to render the expected yields from these two alternatives equal.

EXPECTATIONS AND RISK

The pure expectations model assumes that market participants are risk neutral. Reality usually differs from expectations. A risk-neutral person is not concerned about the possibility that expectations will not prove to be correct so long as favorable deviations of actuality from expectations are as likely as unfavorable ones. Risk in itself is not regarded negatively. (If the expectation is looked upon as the mean of a normal distribution of possible outcomes a risk-neutral market participant is concerned only with the mean of the distribution and not with its variance.)

The vast majority of people are risk-averse. They dislike risk. The possibility of favorable deviations from expectations does not fully compensate for the possibility of unfavorable deviations. Risk-averse investors are prepared to forgo some investment return in order to achieve greater certainty of that return. They are prepared to accept a lower average of the possible future returns in order to avoid the chance of very low (possibly negative) returns on investments. (Risk-averse investors are willing to accept a lower mean of possible returns in order to enjoy a lower variance of those possible future returns.)

Risk can be divided between capital risk and income risk (there are other forms of risk such as default risk but in analysing the term structure of interest rates the relevant forms are capital risk and income risk). Capital risk is the risk that the price or value of the instrument will change. Income risk is the risk that the cash flow arising from the instrument will vary. Some market participants will be primarily capital risk-averse whereas others will be primarily concerned with income risk. An institution whose liabilities are largely short term is likely to be capital risk-averse. Such institutions would include retail banks and building societies. If they matched their short-term liabilities with long-term fixed interest assets, such as government or corporate bonds, there is a possibility that the bonds would need to be sold at a time when interest rates are relatively high. Given the inverse relationship between interest rates and bond prices the sale of bonds at such a time could involve the realization of capital losses. The institutions concerned would be capital risk-averse and would prefer assets whose capital values show little variability. They may be prepared to accept lower interest rates on capital certain assets and, correspondingly, would require higher rates of return on long maturity fixed interest assets as compensation for the sacrifice of capital certainty.

Other market operators would be more concerned with the risk of fluctuations in cash flow. A pension fund may require a series of known cash flows in order to meet its commitments. A life assurance fund manager may intend to hold a security to maturity and would therefore be immune from capital risk, but would be concerned with interim income receipts because of their importance for the build up of the fund. Such market participants might require a premium on the interest receipts from short-term assets in order to compensate for the fact that when an asset matures and the money is reinvested the new interest rate might be relatively low. Conversely, they would accept a reduced interest rate for the advantage of income certainty provided by securities with distant maturities.

Money markets and interest rates

It is not only the holders of assets who are concerned with capital or cash flow risk. The issuer of securities could have parallel concerns. A corporate borrower is likely to prefer the cash flow certainty provided by a long-term fixed interest liability to the uncertainty involved in rolling over short-term liabilities at interest rates that are revised each time. Such a borrower would be prepared to pay an interest rate premium in order to obtain certainty as to financing costs.

The relative capital and cash flow risk-aversion of borrowers and lenders will determine whether long-term rates include a risk premium relative to short-term rates or vice versa. If borrowers wish, on the whole, to incur long-term debt and lenders tend towards capital risk-aversion then long-term debt instruments would need to include a premium in the interest payments so as to induce lenders to provide funds on a long-term basis. Borrowers would be prepared to pay the premium in order to obtain money on terms that are suitable to them. Under such circumstances there would be a tendency for the yield curve to exhibit an upward slope (steeper upward slope or less steep downward slope depending upon the interest rate expectations).

On the other hand, strong income risk-aversion would cause investors to prefer long-term investments. If this was stronger than any preference of debtors for long maturities the short-term interest rates would be at a premium to the long-term rates. Those wishing to borrow short term would need to offer relatively high short-term interest rates in order to induce lenders to accept the income risk of lending short term. This would tend to produce a downward sloping yield curve (less steeply upward sloping or more steeply downward sloping given interest rate expectations). However, the most frequent situation is probably that of borrowers wishing to borrow long and lenders wishing to lend short so that an interest rate premium on long-term instruments becomes necessary in order to induce lenders to lend long.

PREFERRED HABITAT AND MARKET SEGMENTATION

Capital risk-aversion and income risk-aversion imply that market participants do not regard instruments of different maturities as perfect substitutes for one another. Risk-aversion may not be the only reason for poor substitutability and in the extreme, some participants might regard instruments of differing maturities not to be substitutes at all.

Many investors would have preferred habitats in the sense of having an attachment to assets of a particular maturity. Large numbers of people would keep their money in short-term interest-bearing deposits without considering a switch to longer maturity assets whatever happens to the relative rates of return. To the extent that no changes in relative interest rates would induce a move along the maturity spectrum, there is market segmentation. Market segmentation arises from an extreme form of the preferred habitat phenomenon.

An attachment to instruments of a particular maturity range for reasons of preference, regulation or ignorance of alternatives could lead to a situation in which very large differences in interest rates between alternative maturity ranges are necessary to induce investors or borrowers to switch between maturity ranges. If the disposition towards a preferred habitat goes as far as precluding any possibility of using other maturities, market segmentation can arise. If the markets are dominated by investors and borrowers who are unwilling to move outside their chosen maturity ranges, the interest rates for the different maturity ranges would be determined independently. Demand and supply for money or loanable funds in the different maturity ranges would determine the various interest rates independently of one another. The determination of short-term and long-term interest rates would occur through separate processes and the markets for the different maturities would not influence one another.

One of the yield curves depicted by Figure 3.6 is labelled 'walking stick'. This is not an uncommon form of yield curve. Interest rates first rise with increasing maturity, but then show a decline after a particular maturity has been passed. This phenomenon might be explained in terms of separate determination of short, medium and long-term interest rates. Alternatively the short end of the market could be seen as segmented from the long end with the short end being characterized by capital risk-aversion (requiring higher interest rates to compensate for the increased risk of capital loss as the maturity extends) and the long end being characterized by income risk-aversion (investors being prepared to accept lower interest rates for the income certainty provided by very long-term assets).

APPENDIX: IMPLICATIONS OF A FLAT YIELD CURVE

It is tempting to think that a horizontal yield curve implies an expectation of unchanging short-run interest rates, when taking the pure expectations approach. However, even in the absence of a risk premium a horizontal yield curve is suggestive of an expectation of falling interest rates. Consider the case of one-month and two-month rates both being 12% p.a.

Money markets and interest rates

What one-month rate is expected to prevail a month from the present? Two successive one-month rates of 12% p.a. would compound to a sum in excess of that provided by a two-month rate of 12% p.a.

$$(1.01)^2 = 1.0201 > 1.02$$

Two successive 1% returns, when compounded, exceed the 2% return from the two-month deposit. A return of 0.99% in the second month would, when compounded upon the 1% return of the first month, yield the equivalent of a two-month 2% return. The one-month rate of 0.99% is equivalent of an annual rate of 11.88%. (Note that rates are annualized in the short-term money markets by simple multiplication, by 12 and 6 in the present example, rather than by compounding, and hence simple division can be used to derive shorter rates of interest from annualized ones.)

The future rates of interest implied by current ones are known as forward/forward rates. In the present example, a spot one-month rate of 12% p.a. and a spot two-month rate of 12% p.a. together imply a forward/forward rate for a one-month deposit to be made one month from the present of 11.88% p.a. According to the pure expectations approach, the forward/forward rate constitutes the expected future rate. A flat yield curve is thus indicative of expectations of declining short-term interest rates.

Managing interest rate risk by unitizing debt

The period since the mid-1970s has witnessed movements in interest rates that exceed any in living memory. Fluctuations in interest rates pose problems for borrowers and lenders alike. Business planning is severely hampered by uncertainty as to future interest rates, and investment projects might be abandoned since there may be no guarantee that interest on money borrowed to finance the investments will not rise to an extent that renders them unprofitable.

In such a situation, any device that is capable of moderating the cash flow implications of interest rate fluctuations deserves careful attention. It is proposed that unitizing debt can achieve this outcome. Just as assets can be accumulated by purchasing units in a fund, a loan can be divided into units which can be repurchased by the debtor over time.

Under such a scheme, interest would have its impact by way of raising the value of the units. So the effect of a rise in interest rates would be spread over time – unlike conventional debt repayment systems which require the borrower to pay the whole of the additional interest in the current year. The initial impact would be only via those units repurchased in the current year, the remainder of the increase being reflected in a higher price for the units redeemed in the future.

Conversely, a reduction in interest rates would have cash flow implications spread over time, rather than concentrated in the year of the decrease.

Example 3.7

Consider a hypothetical case which compares the conventional servicing of a debt with servicing in the form of redemption of units. £1,000 is borrowed, which in the unitized case consists of one hundred £10 units. The conventional case involves payment of an identical part of the capital each year (£200 at the end of each of five years). The unitized case involves redemption of units at a declining rate (a declining number per year is appropriate since the value of the units rises each year). The rate of redemption (decided upon at the time of borrowing the money) is 25, 23, 20, 17 and 15 at the end of years one to five, respectively. Interest rates turn out to be 5% p.a. during years one, three and five, whereas a rate of 25% p.a. is experienced during years two and four. Table 3.1. illustrates the two payment patterns.

Table 3.1

	Conventional			Unitized		
	Capital repayment	Interest charge	Servicing cost	Value of units	Units redeemed	Servicing cost
Year 1	£200	£50	£250	£10.50	25	£262.50
Year 2	£200	£200	£400	£13.13	23	£301.99
Year 3	£200	£30	£230	£13.78	20	£275.60
Year 4	£200	£100	£300	£17.23	17	£292.91
Year 5	£200	£10	£210	£18.09	15	£271.35

It can be seen that the unitized approach involves much smaller fluctuations in servicing cost than in the case of conventional debt repayment.

A borrower with a unitized loan would be protected from sharp movements in interest rates. To the extent that rates fluctuate around a steady average, unitized loans would serve to considerably dampen the

Money markets and interest rates

cash flow fluctuations. In so far as an interest rate movement is part of (or around) a longer trend, unitized loans would smooth the adjustment to the new average rate. In both cases, there is a reduction in cash flow volatility and the accompanying uncertainty.

Unitized loans can have a further advantage to borrowers in that they are readily amenable to systems that allow borrowers to pay off debts at rates that match their own earnings. Prosperous years could see many units repurchased, whilst less prosperous periods would be marked by a slower rate of redemption of units. Such a system could ease the cash flow implications of debt during periods that are relatively difficult for the borrower. No doubt lenders would wish to insist on minimum numbers of units being redeemed each year, but such minima could readily be incorporated into such systems.

By reducing the destructive effects of interest rate volatility on businesses, a generalized adoption of unitized lending could allow governments to manipulate short-term interest rates for macroeconomic purposes without worrying about the impact of the resulting volatility on business activity. In particular, the use of high interest rates for the control of inflation need not be associated with deep recession and business failures.

Further reading

P.G.A. Howells and K. Bain, *Financial Markets and Institutions* (Longman, 1990).
David Kern, *Interest Rate Forecasting* (Woodhead-Faulkner, 1992).
James C. Van Horne, *Financial Market Rates and Flows* (Prentice Hall, 1990).

4

~

Stocks and bonds

Stock valuation

Investment analysts need to produce estimates of what stock prices should be. Market makers need such estimates for the purpose of generating appropriate quotes and investors need them for ascertaining which stocks are over- or underpriced in the market. There are two major approaches. One proceeds by obtaining estimates of the price–earnings ratio and of prospective earnings. The other discounts prospective future dividends in order to arrive at their present value.

PRICE–EARNINGS RATIOS

The price–earnings ratio, P/E, is the ratio of the price of shares in a particular stock to the earnings (pre-tax profits) per share. There are numerous ways of ascertaining the price–earnings ratio. One is to use the average of past price–earnings ratios for the stock. Another is to discover what factors affect the ratio, and how they affect it. The ratio can then be calculated on the basis of the current values of such factors. A variant of this approach uses regression analysis to produce equations for the determination of the price–earnings ratio. Such an equation might take the form of

$$P/E = 3 + 2(\text{growth rate in earnings}) + 0.5(\text{dividend payment rate})$$

This hypothetical equation states that the price–earnings ratio for a particular stock is equal to three plus twice the rate of growth of earnings plus half the proportion of those earnings that is paid out in dividends.

The price–earnings ratio is then multiplied by current or prospective earnings in order to arrive at an estimate of what price shares in the stock should be.

Stocks and bonds

This approach to stock price valuation uses variations on the discounted cash flow model:

$$P = D_1/(1+r_1) + D_2/(1+r_2)^2 + D_3/(1+r_3)^3 + \ldots + D_N/(1+r_N)^N$$

where $D_1, D_2, D_3, \ldots, D_N$ are the dividends per share of stock expected at points of time in the future. The final point of time, indicated by N, would usually be treated as being infinitely distant. The rates of discount are indicated by r_1, r_2, r_3, r_N. These discount rates might be based on returns on alternative investments, such as government bonds, with some upward adjustment to reflect the fact that riskier investments (i.e. corporate stock) would be required to yield a higher rate of return.

The investment analyst using this approach would need to generate estimates of future dividend payments and also ascertain appropriate discount rates. For the discount rates there would be a source of information, from which to work, in the form of the yield curve. No convenient source of information exists for the formation of expectations of dividends and so the analyst needs to develop a model of future dividend flows.

The simplest approach is to assume that dividends will remain constant at their current levels. It is more usual to assume that dividends will grow. There are several types of growth path that might be assumed. One takes the form of a constant rate of growth. If the rate of growth is denoted by g the model may be described by:

$$P = D/(1+r_1) + D(1+g)/(1+r_2)^2 + D(1+g)^2/(1+r_3)^3 + \ldots + D(1+g)^{N-1}/(1+r_N)^N$$

D is the dividend at the end of the first period (which may be six months or a year) and g is the assumed growth rate per period. By assuming a discount rate that is the same for all future points in time the above model can be rewritten as:

$$P = D/(1+r) + D(1+g)/(1+r)^2 + D(1+g)^2/(1+r)^3 + \ldots + D(1+g)^{N-1}/(1+r)^N$$

If N is treated as being infinitely distant (as it normally is in stock valuation since corporates typically do not have foreseeable termination dates), this latter form of the model can be expressed as:

$$P = D/(r-g)$$

The value of the firm

This is often referred to as the Gordon growth model. (It is to be noted that the model requires r to exceed g and that a constant dividend would generate a stock price of D/r.)

Other models involve dividend growth that is forecast to occur at rates that differ according to the time period. The two-period model assumes growth at an untypical rate for a period after which growth proceeds at a normal or typical rate. If the untypical growth rate is denoted by G, the typical rate by g, and the untypical growth is expected to occur for N periods at the end of which the stock price is p (with the current stock price denoted by P) then the current stock price can be expressed as:

$$P = D/(1+r) + D(1+G)/(1+r)^2 + D(1+G)^2/$$
$$(1+r)^3 + \ldots + D(1+G)^{N-1}/(1+r)^N + p/(1+r)^N$$

The stock price at the end of N periods, p, can be expressed in terms of the Gordon growth model:

$$p = D_{N+1}/(r-g)$$

where D_{N+1} is the dividend at the end of period $N+1$ (which is the first period of normal growth) and is equal to:

$$D(1+G)^{N-1}(1+g)$$

Some investment analysts use three-period models in which the period of untypical growth is followed by a period during which growth changes from the untypical to the typical rate. At the end of the transition period the third period, during which growth proceeds at a normal rate, begins.

The value of the firm

If the firm is entirely financed by ordinary shares (common stock) then its value is the price of a share multiplied by the number of shares in existence. If the firm is financed by both equity and debt (stocks and bonds) then the value of the firm is the sum of the values of the shares and the bonds. If there are other forms of finance, such as bank borrowing, then they too should be included in the valuation of the firm. In other words, the value of the firm is the sum of the values of the various claims on the firm's earnings, which amounts to the value put on the firm by its owners.

It is possible that the composition of a firm's liabilities can affect its value. Such would be the case if the returns on different types of liability had different tax implications. For example, if interest on bonds and bank borrowing could be treated as costs from the tax viewpoint then the use of such financing could reduce the tax liability and result in a lower tax payment by a firm leveraged in this way. The lower tax payment leaves more to be distributed to those with a claim on the firm's earnings and this greater income distribution leads to a higher valuation of those claims, and hence of the firm.

Risk and return

Thus far it has been assumed that the return on assets is the only criterion for assessing the value of those assets. However there is at least one other criterion, namely risk. For a particular rate of return assets with low risk would be deemed more desirable, and hence would be more highly valued, than assets that are seen as very risky. So risk as well as expected return needs to be considered in valuing the prices of stocks and bonds.

RISK AND DIVERSIFICATION

The risk of a portfolio can be reduced by diversifying the portfolio. Risk might be measured in terms of the standard deviation of expected returns, where expected returns encompass both capital gains and dividends (or coupons). If the potential returns are seen as forming a normal distribution of possible outcomes then diversification can narrow that normal distribution, for example, from A to B in Figure 4.1.

The best results from diversification are obtained when there is low covariance between the constituent assets of the portfolio. Low covariance is associated with low correlation between the returns on the assets concerned. The ideal combination of assets for risk reduction would involve assets with negative correlation of returns, that is, high returns on some of the assets occurring when there are low returns on others so that deviations from the norm tend to cancel each other out. However, negative correlations are not normally available (unless financial futures or options are used) and the best that can be usually achieved is low positive correlation. Fortunately, diversification that combines positively correlated assets will still reduce risk so long as the correlation is not perfect. The variance (square of the standard deviation) of a portfolio is given by:

$$Sp^2 = \sum_{i=1}^{N} \sum_{j=1}^{N} X_i X_j S_i S_j R_{ij}$$

72

Risk and return

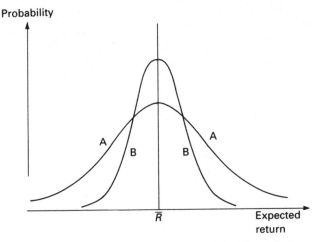

Figure 4.1 Diversification can narrow the normal distribution of possible outcomes

where X_i is the proportion of the portfolio in the form of asset i, X_j is the proportion in the form of asset j, S_i is the standard deviation of returns on asset i, S_j is the standard deviation of asset j, and R_{ij} is the correlation between the returns on assets i and j.

It can be seen that the lower is the correlation between the returns on the constituent assets, the lower is the portfolio variance (and hence risk). It may even be the case that adding an asset that is riskier (on its own) than any of the existing assets (on their own) in the portfolio would reduce the overall portfolio risk since, although the high standard deviation would add to overall variance, a sufficiently low correlation would reduce that variance.

For a particular set of securities available for a portfolio and for a specific expected return (statistical expectation, the most probable return shown by a normal distribution such as those of Figure 4.1) on that portfolio, there would be a combination of the constituent assets that minimizes the portfolio risk (variance and standard deviation). For each possible expected return it is possible (in principle) to ascertain the proportions of the constituent assets in the portfolio that will minimize the overall risk of the portfolio. By finding the minimum risk for each possible expected rate of return an efficiency frontier can be produced. Such an efficiency frontier is illustrated by Figure 4.2.

It would not be rational to hold a portfolio below and to the right (the shaded area) of the efficiency frontier since such a portfolio can be

73

Stocks and bonds

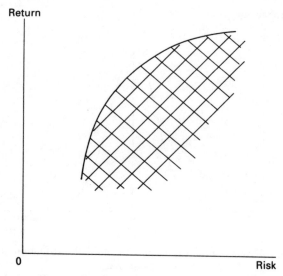

Figure 4.2 An efficiency frontier may be produced based on the minimum risk for each possible return

improved upon by obtaining the same expected return at lower risk or a higher expected return at the same risk. Points above and to the left of the efficiency frontier are not attainable and hence are not feasible. Points in the shaded area are feasible but not efficient since all such points are dominated by points on the efficiency frontier. When a portfolio either yields a lower expected return for the same risk, or a higher risk for the same expected return, as an alternative portfolio then it is said to be dominated by that alternative portfolio.

This approach to portfolio diversification (pioneered by Markowitz) suffers from the practical problem of requiring an enormous amount of information. It requires knowledge of the expected returns on each asset, the standard deviation of those expected returns, and the correlation of expected returns between every pair of assets. When the available assets are numbered in thousands, the data requirements become vast. Fortunately, the data requirements can be greatly reduced by using correlations with stock indices in the place of correlations between individual stocks (an approach suggested by Sharpe).

THE CAPITAL ASSET PRICING MODEL

Thus far it has been assumed that all assets available for a portfolio bear risk. However, some short-term money market assets can be regarded

Risk and return

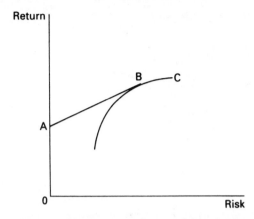

Figure 4.3 Combining riskless assets with a portfolio of risky assets gives a modified efficiency frontier

as (virtually) riskless. Bank deposits and Treasury bills might be seen as riskless since they provide a certain return (over a short period) with no risk of capital loss. Such risk-free assets can be depicted by a point on the vertical axis of Figure 4.2. That point is depicted by A in Figure 4.3.

An investor can choose a portfolio that combines a holding of riskless assets with a portfolio of risky assets. The efficiency frontier then becomes ABC in Figure 4.3. The new efficiency frontier follows the straight line AB before joining the efficiency frontier of the risky portfolio. It is to be noted that an investor choosing to combine riskless and risky assets would find just one portfolio of risky assets optimal, the portfolio at point B in Figure 4.3.

The next step is to introduce the ability to borrow in order to finance a holding of the portfolio of risky assets. The effective efficiency frontier then becomes the straight line ABC in Figure 4.4. Above and to the right of point B the investor borrows in order to buy the portfolio of risky assets. If the rate of interest for borrowing exceeds the rate for lending, as can be expected, the gradient of the straight line for the borrowing would be less than that for the lending – corresponding to a higher point on the vertical axis – and there is no longer a single unique portfolio of risky assets that investors would find optimal to hold.

If an investor chooses to combine the riskless asset with risky assets the resulting expected return will be a weighted average of the return on the riskless asset and the expected return on the portfolio of risky assets.

$$R = R_D + (R_P - R_D)X \qquad (4.1)$$

75

Stocks and bonds

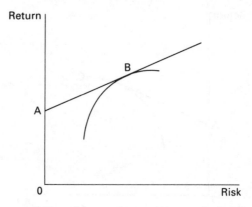

Figure 4.4 The possibility of borrowing to increase the holding of the risky portfolio

where R is the overall expected return, R_D is the return on the riskless asset (e.g. bank deposit), R_P is the expected return on the portfolio of risky assets (at point B in Figures 4.3 and 4.4), and X is the proportion of the total portfolio that is held in the risky portfolio.

Combining the riskless asset with the portfolio at B generates a level of risk that is a weighted average of the two levels of risk. Since the risk on riskless assets is zero the weighted average becomes:

$$S = XS_P \qquad (4.2)$$

where S is the standard deviation of expected returns on the total portfolio and S_P is the standard deviation of expected returns on the portfolio of risky assets.

Equations 4.1 and 4.2 are also applicable to the case of borrowing in order to finance a holding of the risky portfolio that exceeds the value of the total portfolio (which in such a case would amount to the value of the holding of the risky portfolio minus the sum of money borrowed). In this case, the expected return on the total portfolio, and its associated risk, would exceed the expected return and risk on the risky portfolio in the absence of either borrowing or lending (point B in Figures 4.3 and 4.4).

From Equations 4.1 and 4.2, Equation 4.3 can be derived:

$$R = R_D + (R_P - R_D)\frac{S}{S_P} \qquad (4.3)$$

Equation 4.3 shows that the expected return on the total portfolio is a function of the risk (as measured by the standard deviation S of the

76

Risk and return

expected returns on the total portfolio). The cost of raising the expected return is the acquisition of additional risk.

The straight line in Figure 4.4 is often referred to as the capital market line. Equation 4.3 is the equation of the capital market line where R_D is the intercept term and $(R_P - R_D)/S_P$ is the gradient.

Risk on securities can be divided into systematic and non-systematic risk. Systematic risk is the market-related risk, it is the movement in the price (or returns) on an individual stock that is associated with movement of the market as a whole. Systematic risk can be measured by the beta of the stock where beta is defined as:

$$\text{Beta} = \frac{\text{Percentage change in the stock price}}{\text{Percentage change in market index}}$$

The market index would be an index of stock market prices (e.g. S & P 500, FTSE 100, Nikkei Dow, CAC 40, DAX, Hang Seng).

Non-systematic risk is specific to the individual stock or its sector. The non-systematic risk can be eliminated by diversifying a portfolio. A fully diversified portfolio would involve deviations from market movements tending to offset one another, upward stock-specific movements would be cancelled by the downward deviation of other stocks. In measuring the risk for the capital market line only the systematic risk is important since portfolio diversification can eliminate the non-systematic risk. It follows that beta can take the place of risk on the horizontal axis.

Each individual stock has a beta value and it is this beta value that makes that stock's contribution to a portfolio beta (the portfolio's responsiveness to market movements). Since most investors dislike risk (they are risk-averse), a stock that contributes heavily to portfolio risk must yield a high expected return to compensate. Assets with high risk should have high expected returns. The capital market line provides a relationship between expected returns and risk. Using this line to ascertain the appropriate expected return for individual stocks (or portfolios of stocks) provides the security market line. The security market line indicates the appropriate expected return for each beta. High beta stocks should have high expected returns, and vice versa.

RELEVANCE TO THE DISCOUNTED CASH FLOW MODEL AND PRICE–EARNINGS RATIOS

The discounted cash flow approach to investment analysis, described earlier in this chapter, requires a rate at which future values are to be discounted in order to ascertain their present values. The capital asset pricing model suggests that the required rate of return is higher for securities with high risk than for securities with low risk. The rate of return required by investors is the appropriate rate at which future cash flows should be discounted. So the cash flows from high risk assets should be subject to higher rates of discount than the cash flows from low risk assets. It follows that for any given expected level of future returns securities with high risk would tend to be less expensive than corresponding low risk securities.

The low price of high risk assets, for any particular expected flow of returns, would involve a low price–earnings ratio. So whether stock valuation is based on discounted cash flows or price–earnings ratios the capital asset pricing model implies that there should be an inverse relationship between the riskiness of asset returns and the price of the asset.

The capital asset pricing model has been criticized for using only one variable, namely, beta, in the determination of the requisite rate of return. There is evidence that other factors may be important. These factors include firm size, dividend yield and price–earnings ratios. Smaller companies, those with high dividend yields and those with low price–earnings ratios, seem to be associated with relatively high expected rates of return.

Bonds and their valuation

Bonds are fixed interest securities. This means that the income stream does not reflect the profits of a firm. The typical bond pays a constant sum to its holder at regular intervals (normally, annually or semi-annually). Bonds may be issued by governments (in some countries government bonds are alternatively known as gilt-edged securities, or gilts), by private companies (in which case they may or may not be secured against assets of the company), or by financial institutions (which may be quasi-governmental such as the World Bank).

A straight bond pays a fixed coupon at regular intervals over its life and then repays the initial issue price at the end of its life (alternatively known as its maturity date). Bonds come in many varieties. Some of the more important variations include irredeemable bonds, which have no maturity date but may simply continue to pay the coupon forever, index-linked bonds, which relate the coupon and principal to a measure of the price level, and floating rate notes, whose coupon payments vary in line with interest rates. The following exposition will concentrate on straight bonds.

Bonds and their valuation

A bond will have a nominal or par value. This is the sum repayable at maturity and would normally be close to the initial sale price of the bond. Bond prices are often quoted in terms of units of currency per 100 nominal (e.g. dollars per $100 nominal). So if a bond is priced at $96 per $100 par (nominal), $100,000 nominal of that bond would be valued at $96,000.

Bond prices, like the prices of other securities, are determined by supply and demand on the part of investors and borrowers. The primary market is the market in which issuers of bonds (i.e. borrowers) sell new bonds. The secondary market is the market in which existing bonds are bought and sold. The existence of the secondary market means that the buyers of bonds can get their money back (by selling their bonds) before the maturity dates of the bonds. This facility makes the purchase of bonds more attractive.

The market participants need to be able to ascertain the appropriate prices of bonds. This is done by means of the discounted cash flow model. A straight bond has a series of known future cash flows in the form of annual, or semi-annual, coupon payments plus the repayment of principal at maturity. These future cash flows are discounted in order to ascertain their present value, which is the fair price of the bond. The rate of discount will depend upon the perceived riskiness of the bond (risk of default by the issuer). Government bonds are frequently seen as being virtually riskless and hence their discount rates (required rates of return) are relatively low. So for a particular stream of cash flows the prices of such low risk bonds would be relatively high. Corporate bonds vary in their levels of riskiness. Moody's and Standard & Poor's class bonds according to their riskiness, and those rated as relatively risky will have high required rates of return and hence high rates of discount. The riskiest bonds, known as junk bonds, have very high rates of discount and hence sell at relatively low prices.

Another factor affecting discount rates is the timing of the cash flow. If interest rates for distant maturities differ from interest rates for nearby maturities then different rates of discount are applicable to cash flows anticipated at different points in time.

The most common type of bond is a straight bond with semi-annual coupon payments. Using the discounted cash flow model to value such a bond produces:

$$P = C/(1+0.5r_1) + C/(1+0.5r_2)^2 + C/(1+0.5r_3)^3 + \ldots + C(1+0.5r_{2T})^{2T} + B/(1+0.5r_{2T})^{2T}$$

Stocks and bonds

where P is the present value of the bond, C is the half-yearly coupon payment, T is the number of years to maturity, r_1 is the interest rate applicable to six-month assets, r_2 the interest rate for one-year money, r_3 the interest rate on securities with an eighteen-month maturity, and so on. B is the principal sum (nominal value) that is repayable at maturity. The bond to which the equation relates pays out its next coupon in six months from the present.

The fair price of the bond is inversely related to interest rates. Higher interest rates (higher rates of discount) produce lower bond prices. If the bond has no maturity date (i.e. it is irredeemable) and if the yield curve is flat so that the discount rate is the same for all maturities then:

$$P = C/r$$

The bond price is inversely proportional to the rate of discount (and rate of interest). For bonds with maturity dates the inverse relationship is less than proportional. The inverse relationship weakens as the maturity becomes shorter. A bond whose maturity date is imminent will show no price sensitivity to interest rate changes.

MEASURES OF YIELD

The simplest measure of yield on a bond is the current yield (alternatively known as the interest yield or running yield). This is calculated by dividing the coupon on the bond by the price of the bond. So if a bond pays an annual coupon of £9 and has a price of £90 (per £100 nominal) its current yield would be 0.1 (i.e. 10% p.a.).

The price referred to here, and in the preceding discussion of the discounted cash flow model, is known as the dirty price. The dirty price includes accrued interest whereas the clean price does not. Accrued interest refers to the rights to coupon receipts accumulated since the last coupon payment date. For example, a bond with a semi-annual coupon of $4 would, three months after the last coupon payment date, have an accrued interest of $2. A seller of the bond would expect payment for the accumulated coupon rights (the whole coupon will be received by the new holder of the bond) and hence $2 will be added to the clean price in determining the sum payable. Accrued interest will be negative between the ex-dividend date and the coupon payment date. The ex-dividend date precedes the coupon payment date by a few weeks. From the ex-dividend date it is the seller rather than the buyer that receives the dividend. So the seller will receive coupon payments relating

80

to a period during which the bond is not held and receives a correspondingly reduced price upon sale of the bond.

The most frequently used measure of yield is the yield to maturity (otherwise known as the redemption yield). This takes account of the fact that in addition to the coupon receipts there is an element of capital gain or loss from holding a bond to maturity (since the clean price normally differs from the nominal value). The yield to maturity is the rate of discount that equates the future cash flows with the current dirty price of the bond.

This is based on the discounted cash flow model, but instead of solving for the fair price the model is used to solve for the rate of discount that produces a fair price equal to the current dirty price. So for a bond paying coupons on an annual basis and with exactly T years to maturity:

$$P = C/(1+i) + C/(1+i)^2 + C/(1+i)^3 + \ldots + C/(1+i)^T + B/(1+i)^T$$

where the known values are price P, coupon C, principal B, and time to maturity T. The unknown value, for which the equation is to be solved, is the discount rate i. This discount rate is often referred to as the internal rate of return.

The gross yield to maturity (gross redemption yield) is based on the pre-tax value of the coupons whereas the net yield to maturity (net redemption yield) is based on the after-tax value of the coupons.

Yield curves

As shown in Chapter 3 'Money markets and interest rates', a yield curve relates the interest returns on an asset to the maturity of that asset. The most frequently used form of yield curve uses redemption yield as the interest measure to be plotted against the maturity of the financial instrument. However, most financial instruments do not have single maturity dates. The date on which the asset will be redeemed is not the only maturity date. There is also a succession of maturity dates corresponding to the stream of coupon receipts (the coupon payments can be interpreted as a series of minor bond redemptions). For this reason the position of the (redemption) yield curve can vary considerably with the size of the coupon. One way of dealing with this is to use a measure of the average maturity (based on coupon payment dates as well as the final redemption date) as the maturity of the instrument. This measure of maturity is known as duration. An alternative approach is to decompose the receipts from a bond into the stream of coupons on the one hand and the principal to be repaid on the (final) maturity date on the other hand. The rate of return based on the final principal repayment alone has no ambiguity as to maturity date. This rate of return is known as the spot rate. It is alternatively known as the zero coupon or pure discount rate of return, since it corresponds to the return on a bond or bill that pays no coupons, but instead provides a return based on being sold at a discount to its redemption value. A yield curve based on spot rates might be seen as more precise than a redemption yield curve since it does not use misleading measures of maturity.

A potentially very useful yield curve (from the point of view of ascertaining market expectations of interest rates) is the forward yield curve. Such a curve relates future short-term interest rates implied by long spot rates (forward/forward rates) to the point of time to which those implied rates relate. For example, rates of return on five-year bonds and rates on four-year bonds imply rates on one-year instruments to be entered into four years from the present. The implied forward/forward rate can be calculated by means of the formula:

$$(1 + {}_4r_1) = (1 + r_5)^5 / (1 + r_4)^4$$

where r_5 is the five-year interest rate, r_4 is the four-year interest rate, and ${}_4r_1$ is the one-year rate expected in four years' time.

This formula arises from the relation:

$$(1 + r_5)^5 = (1 + r_4)^4 (1 + {}_4r_1)$$

which states that a five-year investment at the five-year interest rate should yield the same final sum as a four-year investment at the four-year rate with the proceeds reinvested for one year at the one-year rate expected to be available four years hence.

Forward interest rates might be looked upon as being marginal interest rates. For example, the current four-year interest rate could be regarded as an average rate (average of the next four one-year rates) whilst the one-year rate for the period commencing four years from now is seen as the marginal rate. If the average rate is rising (the spot yield curve slopes upwards), then the marginal interest rate must exceed the average rate. For instance, if the five-year rate exceeds the four-year rate then the one-year rate expected for four years hence must exceed the four-year rate. Conversely, a downward sloping spot yield curve would involve marginal (that is forward) rates being below the average (that is, spot) interest rates. A five-year rate below the four-year rate requires the interest rate to be pulled down by a one-year rate, expected for four years from

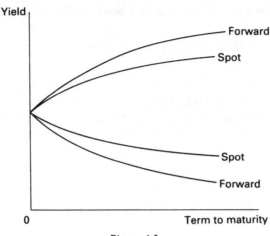

Figure 4.5

the present, that is lower than the current four-year spot rate. So the forward yield curve would be above an upward sloping spot yield curve and below a downward sloping one. This is illustrated by Figure 4.5.

Duration

A coupon-paying bond does not have a single maturity date. Each coupon payment, as well as the final redemption of principal, provides a maturity date. A coupon-paying bond can be regarded as a cluster of pure discount bonds (bonds with no coupon but which simply pay a sum at maturity) with maturities corresponding to the coupon payment dates, in addition to the date on which redemption of principal is to take place. Duration is a measure of the average of these maturities. It is a weighted average of these maturities. It is a weighted average where the weighting is based on the contribution of each receipt of money to the current (dirty) price of the bond. So if a coupon, c, to be received in exactly one year from now has a present value of $V_1 = c/(1+r)$ then its proportionate contribution to the price of the bond is V_1/P where P represents the price of the bond. Its contribution to average maturity (duration) is correspondingly $(V_1/P) \times 1$ year. Likewise a coupon receipt due two years hence has a present value of $V_2 = c/(1+r)^2$ and contributes $(V_2/P) \times 2$ years to the duration of the bond. The principal repayment, B, contributes $(B/(1+r)^T)/PT$ years, where T is the period to final maturity.

83

Stocks and bonds

The equation for the duration of a bond can be written as:

$$D = (c/P) \sum_{t=1}^{T} t/(1+r)^t + (B/P)T/(1+r)^T$$

so each maturity, $t=1$, $t=2$, $t=3$, ..., $t=T$, contributes to duration with the contribution being based on the present value of the money receipts of that maturity as a proportion of the total of such present values (i.e. the price of the bond). The discount rate, r, is the yield to maturity (redemption yield) of the bond.

Sometimes modified duration is used instead. Modified duration is equal to $D/(1+r)$. Duration can be used as a measure of interest rate risk. The present value equation is:

$$P = \sum_{t=1}^{T} c/(1+r)^t + B/(1+r)^T$$

Differentiating with respect to $(1+r)$ gives:

$$dP/d(1+r) = -c \sum_{t=1}^{T} t/(1+r)^{t+1} - BT/(1+r)^{T+1}$$

Multiplying both sides by $(1+r)/P$ gives:

$$(dP/P)/[d(1+r)/(1+r)] = -D$$

This means that (minus) duration is equal to the proportionate change in the bond price divided by the proportionate change in $1+$ redemption yield. It is thus a measure of the responsiveness of bond prices to changes in redemption yields. As such, it is a measure of interest rate risk. The negative of duration might alternatively be interpreted as the elasticity of bond prices with respect to $(1+)$ yield to maturity. It is necessary to use the negative of duration since there is an inverse relationship between bond prices and redemption yields.

It is as a measure of interest rate risk that duration is most useful.

Floating rate notes (FRNs)

A floating rate note is a bond the coupons of which are not fixed but instead varied at points in time, for example, after six-month intervals. The interest rate would be reassessed in the light of a reference rate. Such a bond might, for instance, pay 1% p.a. over LIBOR (London Interbank Offer Rate – the rate of interest at which major banks in

London will lend to each other). Once determined the rate would then be fixed for the appropriate time interval, such as six months.

In many ways, FRNs are similar to short-term money market instruments, such as bank deposits, in that the interest rate is variable. However, the rate is not quite as variable, because once determined it is fixed for a period. As a result of this incomplete variability, a small amount of capital risk persists (as opposed to bank deposits which exhibit no capital risk). If interest rates rise subsequent to an interest fixing date, the fixed rate will seem unattractive and the bond price will fall below par. Conversely, a fall in rates would cause a small enhancement in the value of the bond. This might be looked upon in terms of the yield until the next interest reassessment date being subject to discounting. Of course the price variations would be much smaller than in the case of conventional fixed coupon bonds.

Forecasting

In the Middle Ages alchemists tried to make their fortunes by turning base metal into gold. A modern day equivalent is the attempt to make money by forecasting prices in financial markets. For the most part the level of success is similar to that of the alchemists.

Forecasting is based on either technical analysis or fundamental analysis (sometimes they are combined). Technical analysts look for patterns in the behaviour of prices (in much the same way as fortune tellers look for patterns in tea leaves), sometimes with reference to data on volumes traded. This is alternatively known as chartism. The belief is that prices follow patterns that are frequently repeated such that, if the early stages of a standard pattern can be identified, prices can be forecast to behave in the way suggested by the later stages of that standard pattern. One is bound to wonder why everyone does not seek to make their fortunes by such forecasting if standard price patterns are reliable indicators of future price movements.

Different chartists tend to identify different patterns from the same data set and hence frequently arrive at differing conclusions as to future price movements. This in itself casts doubt on the technique. Of course, those who happen (by chance?) to get the price forecast correct tend to ensure that investors get to know about their success, whereas those who are wrong are prone to keep quiet about it. So one hears about successful technical analysis more often than about failures. Together with the natural human tendency to try to see an order in events, this helps to explain why some people believe in this form of analysis.

Stocks and bonds

An enormous amount of research effort has been put into testing whether price patterns can be used for forecasting. Overwhelmingly, the evidence indicates that they cannot. There are two possible exceptions. The first is the self-fulfilling prophecy. If the number of chartists forecasting a price fall exceeds the number forecasting a rise, chartists would be net sellers. That in itself could cause the predicted price fall. This tendency of prices to follow the predicted path does not mean that the chartists make profits. Many of the sellers would be selling at artificially low prices. This is a recipe for losses. The converse behaviour would be a forecast-induced price rise and resulting purchases at artificially high prices. In these ways technical analysts might induce instability in markets (causing unwarranted price movements), but would tend to incur losses (and go out of business). Such behaviour is sometimes referred to as destabilizing speculation.

The other exception to the rule that technical analysis is of no predictive value, occurs in situations in which governments intervene in financial markets in order to prevent (or induce) particular price movements. The currency markets are most prone to this. One chartist technique is to look for resistance or support levels of prices. These are seen as maximum or minimum prices. If governments are trying to maintain maximum or minimum prices then the chartists' belief in resistance or support levels is well founded. The technical analysis in such circumstances might discover the maximum or minimum price aimed at by the government. A one-way (no lose) speculation opportunity might thereby be identified. For example, buying at the minimum price gives a profit opportunity without a loss potential.

Fundamental analysis is concerned with evaluating all relevant information. In the case of ascertaining the appropriate price for ordinary shares (common stock), fundamental analysis is likely to focus on factors such as the management of the company, its market environment, the general economic outlook and so on. Compared with this type of analysis the chartist practice of looking for standard patterns of price behaviour begins to look like a form of institutionalized superstition.

The efficient markets hypothesis

According to the efficient markets hypothesis, securities prices follow a random walk. A random walk is a pattern of price movements in which one day's price movement is totally unrelated to price movements on

The efficient markets hypothesis

previous days. An implication of this is that recent price patterns (as used by chartists) provide no clues as to future price movements. Also adjustment to relevant information must occur without any lags, otherwise one day's price movement might be part of a lagged adjustment that could be inferred from the previous day's partial adjustment. According to the random walk only new information can cause a price movement. This price movement would take place very quickly (too quickly for profits to be made from the new information) and is equally likely to cause price increases as price falls. The best forecast of tomorrow's price is today's price, however, tomorrow's price will differ from today's in a way that reflects the news occurring between today and tomorrow. That news could be either good or bad.

This leads on to the postulation of three forms of the efficient markets hypothesis. These are the weak, semi-strong and strong forms. The weak form states that present prices reflect all the information contained in previous prices such that there is no profit potential from using historical price data. In other words, chartism is futile. A large number of empirical studies have supported the weak form of the efficient markets hypothesis.

The semi-strong form states that current prices reflect all publicly available information. Publicly available information encompasses not only past prices but also published data on individual companies and the economy as a whole. An implication of the semi-strong form is that there is no scope for making profits from publicly available information since the effect of such information on prices will occur too quickly. A large body of empirical evidence is supportive of the semi-strong form.

The strong form suggests that privately held information is already embodied in prices and hence cannot be used to generate profits from forecasting price movements. Private information can be subdivided into the results of investment analysis which are known only to the analysts (or the fund manager for whom they work) and information arising from having access to privileged information. Use of the latter is illegal in many countries and, not surprisingly, there is evidence to suggest that it can be used to make profits from forecasting prices. As for the private information that is based on investment analysis, it would appear from the empirical evidence (which is based on institutional investors like mutual funds, unit trusts and so forth) that such information is not already embodied in prices, and that as a result it can be used to make profits. Unfortunately, it appears that on average such profits are merely sufficient to cover the cost of the investment analysis.

Stocks and bonds

Appendix: discounting cash flows

A sum of money received (or paid) in the present is worth more than the same sum received in the future. One explanation for this runs in terms of the fact that money can earn interest. A unit of money received now is worth more than the same unit received one year from now because it can earn interest over the year. If the interest rate is 10% p.a., then receipts in the present are worth 10% more than identical receipts one year hence.

To render a future cash flow comparable with a current one the future sum is discounted. This involves dividing the future sum by 1+ the (decimalized) rate of interest. In the case of a receipt of S one year hence when the interest rate is 10% the present value, PV, is given by:

$$PV = S/(1.1)$$

More generally,

$$PV = S/(1+i)$$

where i is the decimalized rate of interest.

If the cash flow is to occur two years from now then (assuming a rate of interest of 10% p.a.) because of compound interest, an identical sum in the present is worth 21% more. The present value would be

$$PV = S/(1.1)^2 = S/(1.21)$$

More generally,

$$PV = S/(1+i)^2$$

Correspondingly, the present value of a sum three years hence is $S/(1+i)^3$, four years hence $S/(1+i)^4$, and so on. It follows that the present value of a future stream of cash flows is:

$$PV = S/(1+i) + S/(1+i)^2 + S/(1+i)^3 + \ldots + S/(1+i)^n$$

where the final receipt (or payment) occurs n years from the present. This can be more formally expressed as:

$$PV = \sum_{k=1}^{n} S/(1+i)^k$$

which states that the present value equals the sum of the discounted cash flows (the cash flow amounting to S at the end of each year) relating to the next n years.

88

Further reading

The time period may not necessarily be a year. If it is not then an adjustment is required to the interest rate. For example, for six-monthly cash flows an interest rate of 10% p.a. would need to be expressed as a rate of 5%.

The cash flow may not be the same at the end of each time period, in which case the equation becomes:

$$PV = S_1/(1+i) + S_2/(1+i)^2 + S_3/(1+i)^3 + \ldots + S_n/(1+i)^n$$

or

$$PV = \sum_{k=1}^{n} S_k/(1+i)^k$$

where $S_1, S_2, S_3, \ldots, S_n$ are the cash flows at the end of periods $1, 2, 3, \ldots, n$, respectively. There may also be a different interest rate (rate of discount) for each time period.

Further reading

David Blake, *Financial Market Analysis* (McGraw-Hill, 1990).

Frank J. Fabozzi and T. Dessa Fabozzi, *Bond Market Analysis and Strategies* (Prentice Hall, 1990).

William F. Sharpe and Gordon J. Alexander, *Investments* (Prentice Hall, 1990).

5

Financial futures

A financial future is a notional commitment to buy or sell, on a specified future date, a standard quantity of a financial instrument at a price determined in the present (the futures price). It is rare for a futures contract to be used for the exchange of financial instruments. Indeed many contracts have no facility for the exchange of the financial instrument. Instead, financial futures markets are independent of the underlying cash market albeit operating parallel to that market. For instance, currency futures are different instruments to the currencies themselves, but currency futures prices move in ways that are related to the movements in currency prices. However, since futures markets are independent of the markets in the underlying instruments this relationship is less than perfect, and it is possible for futures prices to exhibit changes that have no parallel in the underlying currency markets.

The main economic function of futures is to provide a means of hedging. A hedger seeks to reduce an already existing risk. This risk reduction might be achieved by means of taking a futures position that would tend to show a profit in the event of a loss on the underlying position (and a loss in the case of a profit on the underlying position). For example, a borrower who fears a rise in interest rates could take a position in interest rate futures that would show a profit from a rise in interest rates. So the hedger takes a futures position that is opposite to the existing cash market position. Unlike forward contracts, futures typically are not the mechanism for the acquisition of the desired financial instrument. In the case of many futures, including stock index and short-term interest rate futures, there is no facility for acquiring the desired position in the underlying position by means of futures. A short-term borrower would not take out a loan via the futures contract, but instead would borrow in the spot money markets. The futures contracts would have offered protection from an interest rate increase

90

by providing a compensating profit but would be independent of the borrowing itself. The futures would be closed out simultaneously with the borrowing being undertaken, but would have no direct association with the borrowing.

Positions in futures markets can be taken much more quickly and much more cheaply (in terms of transactions costs) than positions in the underlying cash markets. For example, a position in stock index futures can be established within a few minutes (from the time of the decision) at little cost in terms of commissions and bid–ask spreads. The construction of a balanced portfolio of stocks would take much longer and be more costly in terms of commissions and spreads. For these reasons, futures markets tend to be more efficient than the underlying cash markets in that futures prices would be quicker to respond to new information. So futures have a second economic function which might be termed price discovery. Futures prices may be indicative of what prices should be in the markets for the underlying instruments. This price discovery function might be particularly important where the underlying cash market is poorly developed or illiquid, such could be the case in countries with poorly developed financial systems or for instruments that are not frequently traded.

Contracts and exchanges

The largest financial futures exchanges are the two big Chicago exchanges, namely the Chicago Board of Trade (CBOT) and the Chicago Mercantile Exchange (CME). However, most major countries have futures exchanges now. These include the Deutsche Terminborse (DTB), the London International Financial Futures and Options Exchange, the Marché à Terme International de France (MATIF), the Osaka Securities Exchange, the Sydney Futures Exchange (SFE), the Singapore International Monetary Exchange (SIMEX), the Swiss Options and Financial Futures Exchange (SOFFEX), the Tokyo International Financial Futures Exchange (TIFFE – pronounced 'toffee'), and the Tokyo Stock Exchange (TSE).

The most heavily traded financial futures (at the time of writing) are the interest rate futures. These subdivide into the long-term interest rate futures (typically government bond futures) and short-term interest rate futures (typically based on three-month deposits or borrowing). There are also futures contracts on currencies and on stock indices.

Major interest rate futures contracts include the US Treasury bond

Financial futures

(T-bond) contract traded on the CBOT, the eurodollar contract traded on the CME, the Japanese government bond contract traded on the TSE, the Notionnel traded on the MATIF, the short sterling contract traded on the London International Financial Futures and Options Exchange, the US Treasury note (T-note) contract traded on the CBOT, and the 90 day bank bill traded on the SFE.

Long-term interest rate (government bond) futures contracts are based on notional government bonds. For example, a futures contract might relate to a hypothetical government bond with a maturity of twenty years and paying a semi-annual coupon of $8 per year. In the event of such a futures contract being taken to the point at which delivery of bonds is made under the terms of the contract, the seller of the futures contract may choose from a list of eligible government bonds in choosing which to deliver.

Short-term interest rate futures typically do not entail any possibility of delivery. That is, buyers and sellers of the futures contracts are not able to use those contracts for the purpose of making deposits or receiving loans. As will be explained below, profits (or losses) from futures contracts would compensate for divergences between the interest rate actually received or paid, and the interest rate implied by the futures price at the time of buying or selling the futures contracts.

Currency futures contracts typically involve quantities of a currency against the US dollar. Contract sizes might be for example £62,500, DM125,000, and ¥12,500,000. These standard blocks of currency would be traded for US dollars. The futures price is quoted as a price of one unit of the currency in US dollars. If a currency futures contract is taken to maturity such that an exchange of currencies takes place, that exchange will be at the spot rate on the futures maturity date. The difference between that rate and the futures rate when originally acquiring the contract is paid to (or received from) the holder of the futures contract prior to maturity. As in the case of all futures contracts very few currency contracts are held to maturity (the procedures for closing out and receiving profits or losses will be explained below).

Stock index futures provide no facility for delivery and receipt of stock via exercise of the contract. Stock price movements are matched by compensatory cash flows. Futures contracts are available on many stock indices (frequently the index was created for the purpose of futures trading). Stock indices on which futures are traded include the S & P 100, S & P 500, Nikkei 225, FTSE 100, DAX, CAC 40, Hang Seng, Eurotrack and Eurotop. There are contracts relating to all the major stock markets. In the case of the Eurotrack and Eurotop contracts, a number of different national stock markets (in Europe) are covered by a single index and hence futures contract. Contract sizes are based on sums of money per index point. So if an S & P 500 contract is based on $500 per index point and the index (in the futures market) stands at 200 then each futures contract relates to $200 \times \$500 = \$100,000$ of stock. Similarly at £25 per index point a FTSE 100 of 2000 (in the FTSE 100 futures market) indicates that each futures contract relates to $2000 \times £25 = £50,000$ worth of shares.

The margin system

The margin system is central to futures markets. There are three types of margin: initial margin, maintenance margin and variation margin. The initial margin is a sum of money to be provided by both the buyer and the seller of a futures contract when they make their transaction. This margin is a small percentage of the face value of the contract (perhaps 1%). The initial margin is subject to variation (by a clearing house) and will be dependent upon the volatility of the price of the underlying instrument concerned (initial margins might be as little as 0.1% or as much as 10% of the value of the instrument to which the futures contract relates). One function of initial margin is the provision of market discipline. The payment of initial margin may deter poorly capitalized speculators from entering the market.

Whereas initial margin is the sum to be initially deposited (with a clearing house), the maintenance margin is the sum that must remain deposited whilst the futures position is held. Initial and maintenance margins are frequently identical in value. The maintenance margin is returned to the contract holder when the futures contract is closed out or matures. Initial and maintenance margins could be in the form of money (which may earn interest) or other securities (which continue to provide a yield to the holder of the futures position). The maintenance margin will be drawn upon (by the clearing house) in the event of the holder of a futures position failing to make a variation margin payment.

Variation margin is payable and receivable on a daily basis. It reflects the profit or loss made from a futures contract during the course of a day. If the futures price moves to the holder's advantage the holder will receive variation margin, if the futures price moves adversely a payment must be made. This process of realizing profits and losses on a daily basis is known as marking to market. If a contract holder fails to make a variation margin payment, the contract will be automatically closed out and the outstanding sum deducted from the maintenance margin (which is set at a level that is expected to exceed any likely variation margin call).

When a futures deal is agreed between a buyer and a seller, a clearing house takes over the role of counterparty to both buyer and seller. So although buyer A bought from seller B, once the deal is registered the clearing house becomes the seller to buyer A and the buyer from seller B. An implication of this is that there is no need to investigate the creditworthiness of the person or entity with whom a deal is made (the need for such investigation could slow up futures dealing and undermine market efficiency). All default risk is taken by the clearing house. The clearing house protects itself from counterparty default risk by means of the variation and maintenance margins. Marking to market prevents the accumulation of counterparty debt and the maintenance margin is a source from which one day's outstanding variation margin payment can be drawn.

So one implication of the margin system is the removal (or substantial reduction) of counterparty risk. As a result, dealers can feel free to trade instantaneously with any other trader. Another implication of the margin system is that futures are highly geared investments. For example, an initial margin of 1% of the underlying means that the exposure acquired is 100 times the initial money outlay.

Futures funds

Futures funds are collective investments that operate by means of keeping most of their assets in a liquid form such as short-term bank deposits, whilst the remainder is used to finance the margin requirements of futures trading. The gearing offered by futures provides an opportunity for such funds themselves to be highly geared. The market exposure of a futures fund might be several times the value of the fund. Obviously, such highly geared funds are very risky.

Futures funds often contain a wide variety of futures contracts. Multisector funds would not only contain a range of financial futures but also commodity futures, furthermore, the contracts are likely to derive from exchanges in a number of different countries. Such diversification helps to reduce the risk inherent in futures funds. They may be particularly attractive to fund managers since they are likely to exhibit little or no correlation with the assets (such as stocks and bonds) that constitute the major part of investment portfolios. An asset that has low

Hedging

correlation with the other elements of a portfolio will tend to reduce the risk of the portfolio (see the section on risk and diversification in Chapter 4 'Stocks and bonds').

Hedging

Hedging with financial futures entails taking a futures position that is opposite to the position at risk. For example, someone at risk from a rise in interest rates (such as a potential borrower) would take a futures position that would profit from a rise in interest rates. So a rise in interest rates would be compensated by a profit from futures, and a fall in interest rates would be offset by a loss from futures. The hedger attempts to offset any deviation of interest rates from a particular level. The hedger attempts to lock in, or guarantee, a particular rate. Hedging with currency, stock index or government bond futures is based on the same principle.

For the purpose of exposition, short-term interest rate futures will be dealt with at this point. The principles involved are, however, readily extended to other types of futures contract. Short-term interest rate futures are notional commitments to deposit or borrow in the respective currency (futures are available for most major currencies including ECUs). The deposit or borrowing period is typically three months from the maturity date of the futures contract (although some one-month contracts are traded). Short-term interest rate futures are priced on an index basis. The price is 100 minus the annualized (futures) interest rate. So, for example, a futures three-month interest rate of 9.25% p.a. would entail a futures price of $100.00 - 9.25 = 90.75$. By quoting futures prices in this way the inverse relationship between interest rates and prices is maintained. It is to be emphasized that the futures 'price' is not a sum of money that is payable and receivable, it is merely an index.

Futures exchanges stipulate a minimum price movement of futures, this minimum is sometimes referred to as a tick. The tick has a specific money value. For three-month interest rate futures the tick is equal to 0.01% for three months on the sum of money to which a futures contract relates. This sum is (at the time of writing) £500,000 for sterling but 1,000,000 for most other currencies (e.g. eurodollars, eurodeutschmarks, ECUs). So, for example, in the case of eurodollar futures the tick size is $0.01\% \times \$1,000,000 \times 0.25 = \$25$.

A borrower seeking protection from a rise in interest rates would sell futures (note that it is possible to sell futures without having previously bought them). Suppose that the spot three-month eurodollar rate is

Financial futures

8% p.a. and the eurodollar futures price is 91.90 (implying a futures interest rate of 8.10% p.a.). A treasurer anticipating the need to borrow $5,000,000 for three months would sell five contracts. If interest rates rose by 2% so that the spot rate became 10% p.a. and the futures price 89.90 the interest costs of the borrowing would rise by $25,000, but that would be offset by a futures profit of 200 ticks on each of five contracts (i.e. $25,000). A short futures position profits from a fall in price (which enables the seller to subsequently buy at less than the original selling price). If the treasurer no longer required the hedge the short futures position would then be closed out by buying five contracts with the same maturity date as the five originally sold. The short and long futures positions would be deemed, by the clearing house, to cancel each other out leaving the hedger with no remaining futures position. A potential depositor seeking protection from a fall in interest rates would buy futures. A fall in interest rates would entail a rise in futures prices so that the position can be closed out by selling at a higher price.

Short-term interest rate futures relate to deposits or borrowings of three months' duration. If a hedger wishes to hedge a potential deposit or loan of more than a three-month duration, the number of futures contracts needs to be factored up accordingly. The ideal form of hedge is a strip hedge. A strip hedge involves futures contracts with a succession of maturity dates. Most futures contracts, including short-term interest rate futures, have four maturity dates in a year. Typically these dates fall in the months of March, June, September and December (in the case of government bond futures, delivery can take place on any business day in the maturity month, for other contracts, there is a specific maturity date).

Money to be borrowed in September for one year might have an interest rate that will be fixed for that year. Such a one-year interest rate might be looked upon as equivalent to an average of the next four three-month interest rates. Selling futures contracts with maturities in September, December, March and June (and closing all of them out when the money is borrowed in September) would provide the closest approximation to, and the best hedge for, a one-year interest rate. Unfortunately, futures markets sometimes exhibit low liquidity beyond the nearest maturity date (so that for the more distant maturities it may prove difficult to find buyers for the contracts that one wishes to sell). In such a situation a piled up roll may be used. Whereas a strip would hedge a $1 million one-year borrowing by selling one contract for each of four successive maturity months a piled up roll would involve the sale of four contracts for the nearest maturity month.

Determination of futures prices

A user of a piled up roll is vulnerable to a change in the slope of the yield curve. Continuing the example of the potential borrower, a rise in distant forward interest rates not matched by nearby ones (see the section on yield curves in Chapter 4 'Stocks and bonds') would entail a rise in the one-year interest rate without a corresponding rise in the futures interest rate for the next maturity date. In such circumstances, the use of futures with the next maturity date would fail to provide complete protection against the rise in the one-year interest rate. Changes in the slope of the yield curve could even undermine the effectiveness of an attempt to hedge a three-month borrowing or deposit.

Returning to the example of the treasurer expecting to borrow $5 million for three months, it can be seen that a change in the futures interest rate that does not precisely match the change in the spot interest rate would render the hedge imperfect. For example, a fall in the futures price to 90.00 instead of 89.90 would entail a futures profit of 190 ticks per contract instead of 200. As a result the futures profit would have been $23,750 rather than $25,000. The hedge would have been imperfect. The difference between the spot and futures interest rates is known as basis. A change in basis renders a hedge imperfect. One possible cause of a change in basis is a change in the slope of the (forward) yield curve.

It would be useful to hedge against changes in the slope of the yield curve simultaneously with the ordinary hedge (which might be seen as a hedge against a change in the level of the yield curve). Hedging against a change in the slope of the yield curve can be achieved by means of a futures straddle. A futures straddle involves buying futures for one maturity date and selling for another maturity date (obviously this technique requires adequate liquidity for more than one futures maturity).

If the risk is that the slope of the yield curve will become more positive (distant interest rates rise relative to nearby ones) then a futures position must be taken in order to profit from such an eventuality. A more positive yield curve would entail a fall in distant maturity futures prices relative to nearby ones. To profit from such a change the hedger should buy nearby futures and sell the distant ones. Conversely a hedger who would suffer from the yield curve becoming less positive (distant interest rates falling relative to nearby ones) would sell nearby futures and buy futures with a more distant maturity.

Determination of futures prices

Arbitrage is crucial to the establishment of futures prices. Arbitrage can be defined as the pursuit of riskless profits with zero capital outlay (i.e.

any purchases are made with borrowed money). In the case of currency futures the arbitrage that determines futures prices is the covered interest arbitrage which is described in Chapter 2 'The foreign exchange markets' in relation to the determination of forward exchange rates (which should be close to futures prices). The arbitrage that determines short-term interest rate futures prices is based on forward/forward interest rates. Futures interest rates should show little deviation from the forward/forward rates, a substantial deviation would lead arbitragers to borrow via one of them (futures or forward/forwards) and lend via the other in order to obtain a profit. This arbitrage would reduce the extent of deviation so that the available arbitrage profits would no longer exceed the transactions costs arising from the bid–offer (bid–ask) spreads.

The emphasis here will be on the pricing of stock index futures. One reason for choosing stock index futures is that the arbitrage process leaves considerable scope for other determining factors since transactions costs (and risks) are such that the range of possible prices indicated by arbitrage possibilities is a very wide one. Another reason for choosing stock index futures pricing is the similarity of the principles of stock index futures pricing and government bond futures pricing. They are both based on cash and carry arbitrage.

Cash and carry arbitrage involves either buying in the cash market (stocks or bonds) and selling in the futures market or selling (short) in the cash market and buying futures. The futures price should be such that there is no opportunity for profit from such a procedure.

If stocks are purchased and futures sold a financing cost is incurred. Interest must be paid (or forgone) on money used to buy the portfolio of shares. Conversely, the money raised from selling stocks can be put on deposit to earn interest. The shares acquired when buying stock will produce a dividend yield (which constitutes a loss when stock is sold). The absence of arbitrage profits requires the futures price (stock index) to be at a premium (or discount) against the spot stock index so as to compensate for the excess (or shortfall) of the interest rate over the expected rate of dividend yield. So, in the case of buying stock and selling futures, the cost incurred in the form of interest payments must be matched by the sum of expected dividend yield and the capital appreciation guaranteed by the futures premium. The excess of the interest rate over the expected rate of dividend yield is known as the net cost of carry and determines the excess of the futures price (stock index) over the spot stock index.

Deviation of the actual futures price (stock index) from the one thus determined could lead to the opportunity for profitable cash and carry arbitrage. If the futures price were higher than the implied (fair) value buying a portfolio of shares and selling futures should generate a profit. The opposite arbitrage would be suggested by a low futures price. So a high futures stock index would cause arbitragers to sell futures thereby depressing their prices towards the fair value. A low futures price would lead to buying pressure from arbitragers which would tend to raise the price towards the fair value.

However, arbitragers must cover their costs (and compensate for any risks) before they show a net profit. When transactions costs (and risks) are taken into account, the arbitrage that involves selling futures implies a much higher futures stock index than the arbitrage based on buying futures. Transactions costs include bid–ask spreads on both stocks and futures (although bid–ask spreads on futures are usually extremely small), commissions on the transactions in stocks and futures and any tax payable (such as stamp duty in the United Kingdom). These costs could amount to as much as 2% of the value of the underlying position. In addition to requiring compensation for transactions costs, arbitragers may also require a risk premium as compensation for risks incurred. The cash and carry arbitrage is not totally riskless. It requires the establishment of a balanced portfolio of shares simultaneously with acquiring a futures position. Absolute simultaneity is impossible and prices may move adversely while the arbitrage is being constructed. Furthermore, the stock portfolio is unlikely to be identical to the portfolio used to calculate the stock index and hence may have a different beta value (so that their price movements may not be identical). There may also be interest costs on variation margin payments and these would be of uncertain amount. So the arbitrage is not entirely riskless and some profit margin may be required to compensate for the risk.

It follows that cash and carry arbitrage does not determine a single unique futures price. There is a fair price based on net cost of carry (interest rate minus expected dividend yield) but arbitrage may not be worthwhile until the futures price has deviated by more than 2% from the fair price. So arbitrage merely serves to keep the futures price (stock index) within a band of values, sometimes referred to as the no-arbitrage band. The existence of the no-arbitrage band has implications for the mechanism of futures pricing and for hedging strategies. As for the determination of futures prices the no-arbitrage band allows trading based on speculation to play a role.

Financial futures

The role of speculators

Speculators (often alternatively referred to as traders) take risk in the anticipation of making profits. They buy if they expect prices to rise and sell if a fall is anticipated. Speculation is vital for the efficiency and stability of financial markets. In the absence of speculators other users, such as hedgers, may be unable to conduct the transactions that they require.

Suppose that hedgers seek to adopt a net short position. That is, the hedgers wanting to sell futures outweigh hedgers wishing to buy so that, in aggregate, hedgers are net sellers. This would tend to reduce futures prices. This situation provides opportunities for speculators. If the futures price falls below the expected future spot price speculators may buy futures in order to make a profit from a subsequent rise in futures prices towards the expected level. The situation in which a futures price lies below the expected spot price so that the futures price is expected to rise is known as normal backwardation.

Conversely, if hedgers are net buyers of futures then speculators must be induced to be net sellers. To be induced to sell they must expect falling futures prices. This requires the futures price to exceed the expected spot price. This condition is known as contango.

So falling prices induce speculators to buy, thereby moderating the falls. Rising futures prices lead to sales by speculators who would thereby dampen the price rises. So speculation can reduce the extent of price fluctuation and hence render markets more stable. However, price fluctuation would not be eliminated completely. Some deviation of futures prices from the expected levels is required in order to provide the prospective profits that induce speculation. Furthermore, the prospective profits, and hence price deviation, must be sufficient to compensate the speculators for their transactions costs (which are usually very low in futures markets, particularly for those who do not need to use brokers) and for the risks incurred.

So the presence of speculators ensures that hedgers are able to buy or sell futures contracts when they need to and that they do not face prices distorted by demand and supply imbalances. Speculators fill any deficiency in demand or supply.

The behaviour of speculators helps to determine where, within the no-arbitrage band, the futures price will actually fall. In particular, the actual price would be close to the future spot price expected, on average,

Basis trading

by speculators. If it were below this expectation, they would buy thereby pushing the price up, whereas if it were above the expected level they would sell and hence push it down towards the expected price. There would remain some deviation of the futures price from the expected spot price. The direction of deviation would depend upon whether the market exhibited normal backwardation or contango (whether hedgers were net sellers or net buyers). The extent of deviation would be determined by the level of transactions costs and risks for which speculators must be compensated. Anticipated profits must at least provide such compensation and as a result small price deviations from expected values may persist because they provide inadequate profit potential.

Basis trading

Hedgers seek to offset any loss on their exposure by a profit from parallel price movements in the futures market. However, futures prices may not move entirely in line with cash market prices. The arbitrage mechanisms that provide upper and lower limits for futures prices ensure that any divergence between the two price movements would not be extreme. However, the existence of a band of prices determined by arbitrage allows scope for incomplete correlation between cash market prices and futures prices. If the hedge position taken is one that would profit from a fall in futures prices an upward movement within the band could thwart the hedge. In other words, a downward movement of the band of prices could be offset by an upward movement of the futures price within the band, for example, from below the fair price to above the fair price. Such an occurrence would render the hedge imperfect and cause the futures profit to be less than is required (hedge efficiency would be less than 100%).

This risk to the hedger might also be an opportunity. If the hedger were to time the sale of futures contracts so that the futures price is above the fair price at the time of sale, there would be a better than even likelihood of the futures price falling relative to the band. If such a relative fall were to occur then the hedge efficiency would exceed 100% because the fall in the fair price and no-arbitrage band would be accompanied by a fall relative to the fair price, that is, a fall within the band.

Hedgers attempting such timing would be said to be basis trading. A drawback is that the exposure remains unhedged while the hedger waits for the right moment.

Financial futures

A comparison of futures and forwards

Futures and forwards are similar instruments whose prices tend to be very close. There are none the less important differences. Forwards are actual commitments to future transactions whereas futures are notional commitments. Forward contracts are used to effect the end transaction, the parties to the forward contract are the same as the parties to the subsequent exchange of currencies (or subsequent lending). Futures rarely go to the point of delivery of the underlying financial instrument, and if they do the counterparties involved are not the same as the counterparties to the original futures deal. Futures are financial instruments that are independent of the underlying position, albeit with prices that normally correlate with those of the underlying instrument. Futures positions are normally closed out by taking an opposite futures position (e.g. someone who initially sells closes out the short position by buying an equal number of contracts of the same maturity as those sold).

Secondly, forwards are over-the-counter (OTC) instruments whereas futures are exchange traded. OTC products take the form of an agreement between two parties (e.g. the client and a bank). This agreement is not visible to other parties, the market is not transparent. This lack of transparency means that it is not possible to know the prices at which others are transacting. Different clients may get different prices from the banks. Futures markets are transparent. Everyone can see the prices available. The most transparent markets are the face-to-face markets in which all transactors occupy the same trading area (known as a pit). Everyone can see what quantities are being traded and at what prices. Everyone can obtain the same prices, there is no discrimination between different transactors.

Thirdly, forwards can be tailor-made to the specific requirements of a client. The client can specify dates and amounts to be transacted. Futures are highly standardized. Each futures contract relates to a standard quantity of the underlying instrument. Furthermore, only a limited number of maturity dates are available at any time. A high degree of standardization is necessary for market liquidity, that is, for ensuring that the volumes traded are sufficiently high for buyers and sellers to experience no difficulty in conducting their desired transactions. If the standardization was less, for example, through a greater number of maturity dates or a variety of contract sizes, the number of different contracts would be greater and each variety of contract may experience few and infrequent trades. Such inadequate liquidity could reduce the ability of users, such as hedgers, to establish and subsequently close out futures positions.

Case study

International asset reallocation

Objective
A UK fund manager decides to increase exposure to the US stock market at the expense of UK equity investments. It is desired that £1 million of exposure be reallocated immediately with stock selection (for both sales and purchases) to take place during the following two weeks.

It is 20 March and the current price data includes:
June FTSE 100 futures = 2500
$/£ exchange rate = $2.00/£1
June S & P 500 futures = 200

Design a strategy that might be followed and calculate the numbers of futures contracts involved.

Strategy
The UK equity exposure is reduced by selling FTSE 100 futures. The US stock exposure is increased by buying S & P 500 futures. The US dollar currency exposure implicit in a US stockholding is obtained by selling sterling currency futures. The futures positions are progressively closed out as the cash market transactions take place.

Numbers of futures contracts
£1,000,000/(£25 × 2500) = 16 FTSE 100 futures contracts
£1,000,000/£62,500 = 16 sterling currency futures contracts
$2,000,000/($500 × 200) = 20 S & P 500 futures contracts

Further reading

Steven C. Blank, Colin A. Carter and Brian H. Schmiesing, *Futures and Options Markets* (Prentice Hall, 1990).
Alex Carpenter, *Inside the International Financial Futures and Options Markets* (Woodhead-Faulkner, 1991).
Keith Redhead, *Introduction to Financial Futures and Options* (Woodhead-Faulkner, 1990).

6

~

Options

Options are rights to buy or sell specified amounts of financial instruments on, or before, a particular date. A right to buy is referred to as a call option, and the right to sell a put option. There are two other important distinctions, firstly, between European-style and American-style options. European style options can be exercised (the right to buy or sell can be used) only on the maturity date of the option, which is known as the expiry date. An American style option can be exercised at any time up to, and including, the expiry date. It is to be noted that the distinction has nothing to do with geography. Both types of option are traded throughout the world.

The other distinction is between over-the-counter (OTC) options and exchange-traded options. OTC options are the result of private negoti-ations between two parties (typically a bank and a client). They may relate to any amount of any financial instrument and have any expiry date. In other words, they can be tailor-made to the specific requirements of the client buying the option. Exchange-traded options are bought and sold on an organized exchange. They are standardized as to the amount of the underlying instrument, the nature of the underlying and the available expiry dates. Contracts would relate to discrete blocks of the underlying and would provide a limited range of expiry dates. Most exchange-traded options are American-style.

Figures 6.1 and 6.2 show the proceeds from exercising call and put options, respectively, in relation to the price of the underlying instrument (which for the purposes of the present example is taken to be a stock). The strike price (alternatively known as the exercise price) is the price at which the option holder has the right to buy (in the case of a call option) or sell (in the case of a put option). It would be worthwhile exercising a call option only in the event of the stock price exceeding the strike price. It would not be rational to exercise the right to buy at

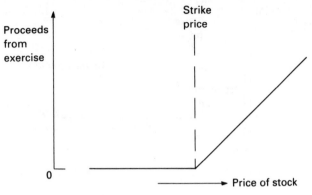

Figure 6.1 Call option

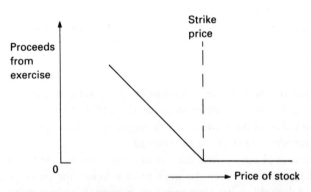

Figure 6.2 Put option

the strike price if the market price is less. Conversely, exercise of a put option would only occur in the event of the stock price being below the exercise (strike) price. It would not be rational to exercise the right to sell at less than the existing market price of the stock.

So, in Figure 6.1 the proceeds from exercise are shown as zero for prices below the exercise price. Strictly speaking the proceeds from exercise would be negative. However, since exercise is not compulsory it is assumed that no one would voluntarily incur a loss, in other words the option would not be exercised and the proceeds would be zero. Likewise in Figure 6.2 the proceeds from exercise are shown as zero for stock prices above the strike price.

If the stock price exceeds the exercise price of a call option, then exercise may be worthwhile. Exercising the option allows the holder to

Options

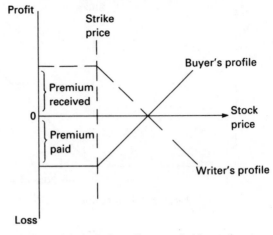

Figure 6.3 Profits and losses of a call option holder and writer at various stock prices

buy stock at less than the market price. The excess of the market price of the stock over the strike price of the call option is known as the intrinsic value of the option (which might be looked upon as the profit from immediate exercise of the option).

In the case of put options there is intrinsic value (scope for profit from immediate exercise) when the stock price is below the strike price of the option. Below the strike price proceeds from exercise (per share) increase one for one with the fall in the stock price. Profit is available from buying shares of stock at the market price and selling those shares at the option strike price by exercising the option.

So options would appear to provide opportunities for profit without risks of loss. For such a desirable position a price must be paid. The price of an option, alternatively known as the option premium, is required by the seller of the option as compensation for taking on the possibility of loss without an opportunity for profit. The option premium is the most that the buyer of the option can lose (this loss would be incurred in the event of the option expiring unexercised) and correspondingly is the most that the seller (alternatively known as the writer) can gain. It must be borne in mind that the buyer and writer of an option are involved in a zero sum gain, the profit of one must be the loss of the other. Figure 6.3 shows the profits and losses of a call option holder (buyer) and writer at various stock prices.

Options as hedging instruments

Contracts and exchanges

In principle the variety of options available in the OTC market is infinite. Whilst the range of different contracts available on organized exchanges is obviously finite it is none the less large, varied and expanding. Exchange-traded financial options are available on stock indices. government bonds, currencies, futures (including short-term interest rate futures) and individual stocks.

At the time of writing the major exchanges for financial options were the Chicago Board Options Exchange (CBOE), the American Stock Exchange (Amex), the Philadelphia Stock Exchange (PHLX), the Pacific Stock Exchange (PSE), the European Options Exchange (EOE), the Australian Options Market (AUS), the London International Financial Futures and Options Exchange, the Swiss Options and Financial Futures Exchange (SOFFEX), the New York Stock Exchange (NYSE), and the Marché des Options Negociables de la Bourse de Paris (MONEP). There are numerous other exchanges and their relative importance (in terms of number of contracts traded) is subject to change.

Options as hedging instruments

The ultimate economic function of financial derivatives (forwards, futures, swaps and options) is to provide means of risk reduction. Someone who is at risk from a price change can use options to offset that risk. A call option can be seen as a means of ensuring a maximum purchase price (if the market price exceeds the strike price then the option may be exercised in order to buy at the strike price). A put option provides a minimum selling price (exercise of the right to sell might occur in the event of the market price being below the strike price). So options can be regarded as means of insurance against adverse price movements.

A hedger needs to compare the use of options with at least two alternatives. Those alternatives are leaving the exposure unhedged and covering it with futures or forwards. Consider a hedger with a long position (such as a holder of stock) who seeks protection from a fall in the stock price. The protection can be obtained by buying a put option. The result is illustrated by Figure 6.4.

The put option protects the hedger from a price fall. Profits from the option offset losses on the stock. However, profits from the rise in the stock price are not offset by losses from the option (apart from the premium paid for the option). So gains are made from a rise in the stock

107

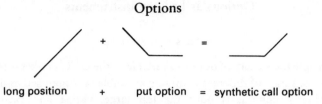

long position   +   put option = synthetic call option

Figure 6.4 Using a put option for protection

price. Thus the net outcome of combining a stockholding with a put option is equivalent to a call option. The combination is known as a synthetic call option.

If the choice is between hedging with the option and not hedging at all the choice is effectively between the long position and the synthetic call option. If the holder of stock is convinced that the stock price will not fall then they would not be prepared to pay a premium for a put option to protect the position from a price fall. At the other extreme, if the hedger felt certain that the price would fall they would either sell the stock or cover it completely by an offsetting short position (in markets where futures or forwards are available the short position can be achieved by selling futures contracts or selling forward). The exposure to the price movement is thereby eliminated completely.

It follows that options would be used only when there is uncertainty as to the direction of price movement. Even then futures or forwards (or selling stock) would be preferable if the hedger believes that the balance of probabilities is that the stock price will fall. The option becomes a possible choice if the hedger either has no view as to future price movements or believes a rise to be the more likely. As illustrated by Figure 6.4 hedging a stockholding with a put option effectively creates a call option. The hedger should construct such a position only if prepared to buy a naked call option (that is a call option that is not used for hedging an existing exposure). Option premiums tend to be such that they match the (statistical) expectations of profit from holding the options. The statistical expectation is based on possible profits weighted by their probabilities of occurrence. If the hedger believes that the stock price is more likely to rise than fall then that hedger would value the option more highly (because of the high probability of profits) than the market (which bases option premiums on stock price rises and falls having equal probability).

So it would appear that a hedger would use options only in the event of believing that the stock price movement is uncertain but more likely to be favorable than unfavorable. There may be other factors impinging on the decision. There is attitude to risk. If a hedger is strongly risk-averse

108

Long versus short option positions

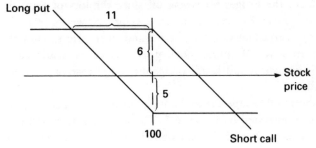

Figure 6.5 Comparison of long put and short call options

then the position would either be liquidated or covered with forwards or futures. Use of options involves some risk, even if it is only the risk of losing the premium paid for the option. An importer may use options to hedge against a rise in the currency of invoice rather than futures or forwards so as to profit from a beneficial currency movement. Hedging with futures or forwards would not provide gain from a beneficial exchange rate movement. Since any unhedged competitors would gain, the competitive position could thus be undermined.

Long versus short option positions

Hedging against a price fall can be carried out by buying a put option and protection against a price rise can be obtained from the purchase of a call option. Alternatively, a call option might be written (sold) as a means of protection from a price fall or a put option written as a means of hedging against a price rise. Writing options is the better approach if the price change is relatively modest, whereas buying options is the more effective strategy in the event of a substantial movement in the price of the stock (or other financial instrument being hedged). Figure 6.5 compares the purchase of a put option with the sale of a call option.

In the example illustrated by Figure 6.5, the two options have the same exercise price of 100. The put is priced at 5 and the call at 6. The long (i.e. purchased) put provides protection against a fall in the stock price below 100, but considering the premium of 5 the put option does not confer a net advantage over an unhedged position until the stock price has fallen below 95. So the long put is beneficial in the event of a substantial price fall.

By writing the call for 6, a premium receipt is obtained and that receipt can be seen as providing downside protection. A stock price fall to 94

109

would leave the hedger no worse off since the loss of 6 on the stock would be offset by the premium receipt. However, the downside protection is constant in money terms and stock prices below 94 would entail a net loss. Of course stock prices above 94 would entail a net profit. So the short call is advantageous in the case of a modest stock price fall.

The short call is superior to the long put down to a stock price of 89. This is demonstrated by Figure 6.5. The net profit from the put option does not exceed that of the call option until the stock price has fallen sufficiently to generate an intrinsic value for the put option of 5 (to offset the put premium) plus 6 (to match the call premium). So the short option position is superior to the long option position until the stock price has moved by the sum of the two option premiums. In this case a hedger seeking protection from a price fall but anticipating a fall of less than 11 would prefer the short call whereas a hedger fearing a greater fall would buy a put option.

Zero cost options

Buying an option involves paying a premium whereas selling an option gives rise to the receipt of a premium. Zero cost options are instruments that can be broken down into constituent options. They consist of long option positions financed by the sale of other options. They can be subdivided into participating forwards and range forwards.

All the constituent options in a participating forward have the same strike price. For the purpose of hedging against a price fall a purchase of out-of-the-money puts could be financed by the sale of a smaller number of in-the-money calls (in other words, the stock price is greater than the strike price). The resulting configuration could be as illustrated by Figure 6.6.

The put options would completely cover the hedger against a price fall whereas the call options would not fully negate the benefits of a price

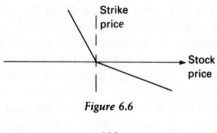

Figure 6.6

The effects of gearing

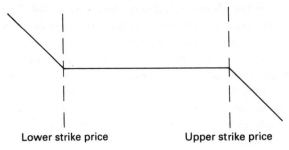

Lower strike price   Upper strike price

Figure 6.7 Range forward zero cost option

rise. So the net effect is that of a forward contract that allows some participation in the benefits of a price rise. (At first sight this strategy may seem to offer benefits without costs. Alas benefits must be paid for, in this case by way of the strike price being below the stock price – so the guaranteed selling price is unfavorable.)

The other form of zero cost option has a number of names including range forward, cylinder and split-synthetic. The constituent options have different strike prices. A price fall could be hedged against by buying a put option with a strike price below the stock price and financing its purchase by writing a call option with a strike price above the stock price. This has the advantage of allowing some profit from a rise in the stock price (up to the strike price of the call option) but at the cost of having no protection against a price fall until the stock price reaches the strike price of the put option. A range forward is illustrated by Figure 6.7.

The effects of gearing

Options can be looked upon as either low-risk or high-risk instruments. In both cases the interpretation of risk is based upon the gearing effect offered by options. An option can be bought for a fraction of the price of the stock (or currency or bond or stock portfolio) to which the option relates. The maximum loss from buying stock is the price of that stock, whereas the maximum loss from buying a call option on that stock is the option premium. So buying a call option on 100 shares of stock can be seen as less risky than buying 100 shares of stock. (The number of shares to which an option contract relates varies from country to country, for example, at the time of writing one option contract related to 1,000 shares in the United Kingdom, 100 in the United States and 50 in Germany.)

111

However, if the choice is between investing $1,000 in stock and spending $1,000 on stock options, then the options appear to be the more risky. Again this arises from the gearing offered by the options. Since the price of the option is a fraction of the price of the stock, percentage changes in the option price are prone to be much greater than percentage changes in the stock price. Suppose that XYZ stock is priced at 100 and a call option to buy at 100 is priced at 5. A rise in the stock price to 110 might plausibly cause a rise in the option price to 13. The stock price rises by 10% whereas the option price rises by 160%. This arises from the gearing offered by the option. However, the possibility of high percentage profits is accompanied by potential large percentage losses. A fall in the stock price to 90 might cause a fall in the option price to 3. The 10% fall in the stock price is accompanied by a 40% drop in the option premium (and hence a 40% loss on the option). It may be that a more substantial fall in the stock price, say to 75, virtually eliminates the value of the option so that a 25% fall in the stock price brings about a 100% fall in the option price. So if the choice is between $1,000 invested in stock and $1,000 in options the latter is the more risky (as usual higher potential profits are accompanied by greater risk).

The foregoing example involved an at-the-money option gaining just 8 in value as a result of the stock price rising by 10. One might think that the right to buy at 100 should rise in price by 10 as a result of a rise in the stock price from 100 to 110. However, although there is an additional 10 in intrinsic value the other component of the option premium, known as time value, falls as the stock price moves away from the option strike price (the initial option price of 5 was entirely time value, at the stock price of 110 the time value of the option is 3). The change in the option price as a proportion of the change in the stock price is known as the delta of the option (in the present example the delta is $(13-5)/10=0.8$).

Determinants of option prices (premiums)

Option prices can be divided into two components, the intrinsic value and the time value. For an American-style option the intrinsic value is the gross profit available from immediately exercising the option and is equal to the difference between the price of the stock (or currency or bond or future or stock index) and the strike price of the option. The option premium minus the intrinsic value is the time value. The time value can be looked upon as a payment for the possibility that intrinsic value will increase.

Determinants of option prices

Time value is affected by the volatility of the stock price. If the stock price is likely to show substantial movements (in either direction) there is an enhanced chance that considerable intrinsic value will accrue prior to the expiry of the option. So greater stock price volatility is associated with higher option prices. Time value (and hence option prices) also tends to be higher when there is a long time remaining before the expiry date. A long time to expiry gives more opportunity for a high intrinsic value than at-the-money options.

A third major influence on time value is the closeness of the stock price to the option strike price. Time value is at its highest when an option is at-the-money (that is when the stock price equals the strike price). Time value declines as the stock price deviates from the strike price (in either direction). If an option is out-of-the-money then the stock price needs to move to the strike price before the option can start acquiring intrinsic value. In consequence out-of-the-money options have less time value than at-the-money options.

Even in-the-money options have less time value than at-the-money options. That is because in-the-money options already have some intrinsic value and that intrinsic value could be lost as a result of an adverse stock price movement. The vulnerability of the existing intrinsic value is compensated for by a reduced time value (lower payment for the possibility of increased intrinsic value).

The option premium could be seen as a means of compensating the writer of the option for the possibility of loss arising from exercise of the option. Each possible level of loss to the writer (profit to the buyer) is weighted by its probability of occurrence. Adding up the values obtained provides a theoretical value of the option. The probabilities are derived from a (log) normal distribution of possible stock prices. The greater the (expected) volatility of the stock price and the longer the time to expiry, the more dispersed the distribution will be. A more dispersed distribution (greater variance) will entail higher probabilities of relatively extreme values and in consequence the weighted sum of potential losses to the writer will be greater. So the option price would be expected to rise with increasing volatility and time to expiry.

An alternative approach to ascertaining theoretical option prices is to assess the cost of hedging the option. Consider a European-style call option on a stock with a strike price of 100. The writer of such an option might hedge any risk by buying the stock whenever its price rises above 100 and selling when the price falls below 100. If the option is in-the-money and hence exercised on the expiry date the writer of the option makes a loss on the option that is offset by a profit on the purchase

113

of stock. In effect, the option writer creates a synthetic option by buying or selling stock as the stock price passes the option strike price.

The cost of this strategy lies largely in the fact that the synthetic option involves buying the stock after its price has risen (and hence at a relatively high price) and selling when the stock price falls (receiving a relatively low price). Buying at high prices and selling at low prices is a procedure that incurs losses. Transactions costs such as bid–ask spreads and commissions increase such losses. The option premium can be seen as compensation for such losses. These losses would tend to rise with stock price volatility and the time period involved. Consequently option prices would be expected to be greater when volatility is high and time to expiry is long.

Minimum option prices

Here minimum will be taken to mean the option price exclusive of time value. Such minimum values constitute theoretical limits below which option premiums should not fall (opportunities for profitable arbitrage would arise in the event of these limits being breached, and the pursuit of the arbitrage profits should ensure that the option prices would at least equal their minimum values). In the case of American-style options the minimum prices would appear to be the intrinsic values of the options. In the case of call options this would be zero if the option is out-of-the-money and the excess of the stock price over the strike price if it is in-the-money. In the case of put options it would be zero for out-of-the-money options and the excess of the strike price over the stock price for in-the-money options. In other words, the minimum values would seem to be the profits available from immediate exercise of the options.

European-style options do not permit immediate exercise unless the expiry date has been reached. In the case of such options the strike price cannot relate to the present but can only be a future value (relating to the expiry date). This future value needs to be discounted in order to render it comparable with the current stock price. So the minimum price of a European call option is either zero or the excess of the stock price over the discounted strike price (that is, the stock price minus the present value of the strike price). Correspondingly the minimum premium for a put option is either zero or the excess of the discounted strike price over the stock price.

The minimum price of a European call option is either zero or the stock price minus the discounted strike price. Above it was said that the minimum price for an American call option would appear to be zero or the excess of the stock price over the strike price. This is less than the minimum price of the European call. However, American-style options must be worth at least as much as European-style options since they offer everything that European-style options offer plus the opportunity to exercise before the expiry date. It follows that the minimum value of an American-style call option is either zero or the excess of the stock price over the discounted strike price.

Exotic options

Exotic option is a generic name that refers to variations on the basic option theme. The following is an indicative, rather than an exhaustive, list of exotic options.

Lookback call options give the right to buy at the lowest price achieved during the life of the option. Lookback put options provide the right to sell at the highest price attained by the underlying instrument.

Asian options involve the average experienced price of the underlying taking the place of the spot price in ascertaining intrinsic value. So European options use the spot price on the expiry date, American options use any spot price observed during the life of the option, and Asian options use the average spot price during the life of the option.

Knock-in and knock-out options either come into being or cease to exist when particular prices of the underlying are reached. For example, down-and-out call options cease to exist if the price of the underlying instrument falls below a particular value. Such options tend to be cheaper than ordinary options.

Options on options may prove useful in certain circumstances. For example, a company tendering for a contract may take out an option to buy an option on the date on which the contract is due to be awarded. (An option would be preferable to a forward or futures position when the contract is awarded if the view is that currency movements are likely to be beneficial but some downside protection is desirable. In other words, the view is taken that the currency of the receivables will probably, but not certainly, rise against the base currency. Options, unlike forwards and futures, allow for profits from such a rise. If the beneficial currency movement is expected with certainty hedging would seem inappropriate. An expectation of a detrimental currency movement would most likely lead to hedging with a forward or futures position – there would be little enthusiasm to pay a premium for the ability to profit from a currency movement that is not expected to occur.)

An option on an option is likely to be cheaper than the substantive option. Firstly, the intrinsic value of an option on an option will be less than the intrinsic value of the substantive option because the delta of the substantive option would be less than one. Secondly, the volatility of an option price will be less than the volatility of the underlying instrument (again because the option delta will be less than one). Thirdly, if the option on an option has a shorter period to expiry than the substantive option – as is likely to be the case – the time value of the option on the option will be relatively low as a result.

Notational formulations

The minimum value of an American-style call option can be expressed as

$$C = \max(O, S - K)$$

If the option is in-the-money the minimum value is $S-K$, the excess of the spot price over the exercise price. (Since an American call must be at least equal in value to a European call this expression should, strictly speaking, use the discounted strike price in the place of the strike price. However, for the purposes of the following discussion this refinement can be ignored.) If the option is at- or out-of-the-money, its minimum value is zero. So the minimum value of a call option is the greater of zero and the excess of the spot price of the underlying over the exercise price of the option.

The minimum value of an American-style put option can be stated as:

$$P = \max(O, K - S)$$

The minimum price of a put option is the greater of zero, and the exercise price minus the spot price. In other words, the minimum value is the intrinsic value and the intrinsic value cannot fall below zero.

The above notation can be used to describe exotic options. For example, lookback call options give the right to buy at the lowest price attained by the underlying instrument during the life of the option. In other words, the exercise price will be equal to the lowest price achieved by the underlying. In notation form:

$$C = \max[O, S_n - \min(S_0, S_1, \ldots, S_n)]$$

Notational formulations

S_0, S_1, etc., are the observed prices of the underlying where the subscripts denote successive points in time. The minimum price of the call option is the highest of zero and the excess of the spot price over the exercise price. The spot price is the terminal price of the underlying, S_n, whereas the exercise price is the lowest spot price observed during the life of the option, that is $\min(S_0, S_1, \ldots, S_n)$.

A lookback put option gives the right to sell at the highest observed price. In other words, the highest observed price becomes the exercise price.

$$P = \max[O, \max(S_0, S_1, \ldots, S_n) - S_n]$$

The intrinsic value of an in-the-money put option is the exercise price, that is, $\max(S_0, S_1, \ldots, S_n)$, minus the spot price at the time of exercise, S_n.

Average strike options have strike prices that are an average of the actual spot prices experienced during the life of the option. In notation form:

$$C = \max\{O, S_n - [\Sigma S_i/(n+1)]\}$$
$$P = \max\{O, [\Sigma S_i/(n+1)] - S_n\}$$

The strike price is $\Sigma S_i/(n+1)$ where ΣS_i is the sum of the observed spot prices (at points of time $i = 0,1,2,\ldots,n$) and $n+1$ is the number of observed spot prices. S_n is the spot price of the underlying at time n, which is the moment at which the option is exercised or at which it expires.

Asian options (average price options) involve the average observed price taking the role of the spot price in determining the minimum value (intrinsic value) of the option.

$$C = \max\{O, [\Sigma S_i/(n+1)] - K\}$$
$$P = \max\{O, K - [\Sigma S_i/(n+1)]\}$$

Down-and-out call options can be looked upon as conditional options. They behave like normal American-style call options so long as the price of the underlying remains above a particular level. In notation form:

$$C = \max(O, S_n - K) \text{ if } \min(S_0, S_1, \ldots, S_n) > H \text{(where } H < K)$$
$$C = O \text{ if } \min(S_0, S_1, \ldots, S_n) \leqslant H$$

So long as none of the observed spot prices $(S_0, S_1, \ldots, S_n)$ falls to H (which is below the exercise price K) the option behaves in the same way as a normal call. If the price of the underlying declines to H or less, the option ceases to exist.

Correspondingly, there are down-and-in calls that come into existence

Options

only if the price of the underlying falls to, or beyond, a specific value. Down-and-out puts (otherwise known as up-and-out puts) cease to exist if the price of the underlying rises to a particular level, which is greater than the exercise price. Up-and-in puts come into existence when the price of the underlying rises to a particular level.

Compound options, which are options on options, can also be described using notational form. For a call on a call:

$$C = \max[O, \max(O, S_n - E) - K]$$

The option on the option has an exercise price of K, whereas the option whose price (or minimum value) constitutes the price of the underlying for the option on it has an exercise price of E. In the case of a call on a put the expression is:

$$C = \max[O, \max(O, E - S_n) - K]$$

A put on a call would be:

$$P = \max[O, K - \max(O, S_n - E)]$$

whereas a put on a put could be described by:

$$P = \max[O, K - \max(O, E - S_n]$$

This is not an exhaustive list of exotic options; however, it is indicative of the range of such options. Furthermore, in order to avoid excessive complexity, time value has been ignored. The notation has been concerned solely with intrinsic values, in other words, minimum values.

The discussion has thus far largely ignored potential uses of the exotic options. It is difficult to be prescriptive about potential uses since it is impossible to foresee every possible circumstance. However, some suggestions might be provided.

Lookback options could be useful for a fund manager who expects a stock price to temporarily reach a particularly high or low level during the lifetime of the option. Average strike options might be attractive to an importer seeking to ensure that the purchase price of foreign currency is in line with the average purchase price faced by that importer's competitors. Asian options are useful for those who make frequent purchases or sales of the underlying, and hence experience a variety of spot prices. Hedgers would use Asian options to obtain compensation in the event of average purchase prices being too high or average sale prices being too low. The conditional options (down-and-outs, etc.) are a means of reducing the costs of options, such options would tend to be relatively cheap because they exclude some profit possibilities. Compound options might also be regarded as a means of reducing costs using options, particularly when a contingent risk is being hedged. An exporter tendering for a contract in foreign currency might want an option to buy another option with a view to exercising the option on an option in the event of the tender being successful. The option on an option could be much cheaper than the underlying option, particularly if it has a much shorter time to expiry (that is, the time to the acceptance of the tender is much less than the subsequent period to the payment for the project). This reduction of initial financial outlay on the hedging instrument could be carried further by making the option on an option conditional upon success of the tender (that is, it could have no intrinsic value in the event of the tender being rejected).

Warrants

Warrants are long-term options. They may have expiry dates that lie five years or more in the future (in contrast to stock options which often have a maximum life of nine months).

Most warrants are issued by the company upon whose shares they are based. If they are exercised the company will issue new shares. So, unlike options, warrants are usually used as a means of raising corporate finance. The issuing company receives the money from the sale of the warrants and subsequently receives the money paid upon exercise. In contrast to options, warrants tend to entail the expansion of the number of shares in issue.

Warrants are often attached to company debt, such as loan stock, when they are issued. The presence of such warrants renders the debt more attractive to the investor, and hence the issuing company can raise money on more advantageous terms in that they need pay a lower rate of interest than would otherwise be the case. In most instances, the warrant is detachable from the host debt instrument and can be traded in its own right. Some warrants are issued naked, in other words, without the presence of corporate debt instruments. Since warrants normally pay no dividend or coupon they provide an issuing company with a source of finance that involves no initial servicing costs.

Some warrants are not connected with the raising of corporate finance. Third party warrants (sometimes misleadingly named 'covered' warrants) might be written by a bank without any involvement of the company on whose stock the warrants are based. One type of third party warrant

Options

is, however, used for the raising of corporate finance. This involves the company that is raising the finance issuing warrants on the stock of another company.

Convertibles

A convertible might be looked upon as a corporate bond with an attached call option. Convertibles are often referred to as convertible loan stock (or convertible unsecured loan stock since most are unsecured) and involve the right to convert the loan stock into shares at specified rates and points of time. Convertible preference shares are preference shares with the right to convert to ordinary shares. Some convertibles provide the right to convert to other loan stock rather than shares.

The number of shares for which the bond can be exchanged is referred to as the conversion rate. So, for example, the convertible may allow the conversion of £100 par value of loan stock into 20 shares. Multiplication of the conversion rate by the share price provides the conversion value. A share price of £6 would imply a conversion value of £120. Convertible loan stock would also exhibit an investment, or straight bond, value. This is the value of the bond (or preference share) in the absence of the right to convert. The investment value is the price of a corresponding straight bond or preference share.

The market value of the convertible would normally be higher than the greater of the conversion and investment values. The excess of the market value over the greater of the conversion or investment value is often referred to as the premium. Figure 6.8 illustrates the relationship between the conversion, investment and market values of a convertible.

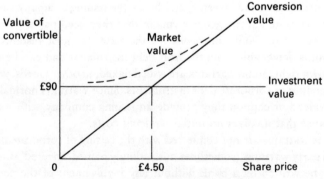

Figure 6.8 Convertible loan stock

It is assumed that the conversion rate is 20 and that the investment value is £90 per £100 par value.

Figure 6.8 illustrates the convertible as a loan stock with an attached option. The investment value is that of the naked loan stock whilst the excess of the market value over the investment value corresponds to the option premium. In this example, the option has a strike price of £4.50. The excess of the conversion value over the investment value corresponds to the intrinsic value of the option.

It must be realized that the investment value, and hence the strike price of the implicit option, is not immutable. A rise in interest rates would lower the investment value and strike price. Similar effects would arise from a decline in the credit standing of the company, such a decline requiring a higher rate of return which, given a constant coupon or dividend, implies a fall in the price of the loan stock (or preference share).

Convertibles are hybrids in that they constitute a compromise between bonds and shares. They provide more upside exposure to share price movements than bonds but less than ordinary shares. They provide less downside protection than bonds, but more than shares. The percentage rate of dividend or coupon yield would be less than that of a straight bond (because the market value exceeds the investment value), but probably more than that of the ordinary share (a rate of dividend yield on the share that exceeds the rate of coupon yield on the convertible would probably induce conversion of the convertible into the share).

The fact that the convertible involves a lower rate of coupon yield than a straight bond renders it attractive to the issuer. The attached option causes the investor to require a lower coupon yield. Convertibles thus provide a cheaper source of finance than loan stock or preference shares. Their advantage over ordinary shares, from the point of view of the issuer, is that they constitute a form of deferred equity. In particular, the voting rights do not accrue to the holder until conversion takes place.

Holders of a convertible have the right to convert during a conversion period. If conversion does not take place during that period the convertible might simply become a loan stock or preference share. So, for example, a convertible might offer the right to convert on June 1st of the sixth, seventh, eighth, ninth or tenth years of its life and if conversion does not take place on any of those dates it then becomes unsecured loan stock maturing at the end of a life of a further ten years at which point it would be redeemed at par. The conversion rate would normally imply a high purchase price of the share (if acquired through conversion) on the issue date of the convertible so that a significant share price advance would be necessary for conversion to become worthwhile. It is to be noted that this conversion price per share, based on the issue price of the convertible, is not the same as the strike price of the implicit option as illustrated in Figure 6.8 (which is based on the investment value). The conversion price is the market value of the convertible divided by the number of shares obtained upon conversion. At the time of issue, the conversion price will be greater than the share price.

The price of the option component of the convertible is determined in the same way as the price of any other option. Its value is influenced by time to expiry, volatility, interest rates and the share price in the same way as other options. However, the strike price will be variable since it is dependent upon the investment (straight bond) value of the convertible. The investment value of the convertible is influenced by interest rates and the credit standing of the issuing corporation.

The question arises as to why the holder of a convertible would exercise the right to convert since it might be expected that the market value would exceed the conversion value so that sale of the convertible would appear to be preferable to conversion. The circumstances in which conversion would take place are:

(a) call by the issuing corporation,
(b) the existence of a final conversion date, or
(c) the dividend yield of the share rising above the coupon yield of the convertible.

Sometimes the issuer of the convertible has the right to call it. This means that the holder must either accept redemption of the convertible (probably at the par value of the loan stock) or convert it into shares. If the latter provides the greatest value, conversion will take place.

It was pointed out earlier that the market value of the convertible would normally exceed the greater of the investment and conversion values. This excess corresponds to the time value of the implicit option. When the final conversion date passes, the implicit option disappears leaving only the investment value of the convertible. If the conversion value exceeds the investment value on the final conversion date it would be rational to exercise the right to convert.

The excess of the conversion price over the share price, when expressed as a percentage of the share price, is known as the conversion premium.

$$\text{Conversion price} = \frac{\text{Market value of convertible}}{\text{Number of shares on conversion}}$$

Convertibles

$$\text{Conversion premium } (\%) = \frac{\text{Conversion price} - \text{share price}}{\text{Share price}} \times 100$$

In most circumstances the conversion premium would be positive, corresponding to the time value of the implicit option. However, a time may come when the dividend on the share exceeds the coupon on the convertible (the coupon is fixed whereas the dividend is likely to rise over time.) If conversion dates are at distant intervals (such as a year apart), the prospect of a lower rate of yield on the convertible than on the share could render it less valuable than the shares into which it might be converted. So a share dividend above the coupon of the convertible together with a long time before the next conversion date could entail a negative conversion premium. The prospect of a negative conversion premium subsequent to a conversion date could lead to conversion on that date.

Case study

Hedging with currency options
It is May 7th. The spot price of sterling is $1.7270–1.7280. The prices of sterling currency options on the Philadelphia Stock Exchange are as shown in the Table 6.1.

Table 6.1 Philadelphia Stock Exchange £/$ options: £31,250 (cents per £1)

Strike price	Calls				Puts			
	May	Jun	Jul	Sep	May	Jun	Jul	Sep
1.625	—	9.50	9.58	9.79	—	0.46	1.06	2.30
1.650	—	7.10	7.49	7.83	—	0.87	1.66	3.10
1.675	—	5.24	5.69	6.19	—	1.50	2.49	4.12
1.700	2.43	3.62	4.15	4.83	0.27	2.41	3.51	5.36
1.725	0.84	2.40	2.94	3.69	1.28	3.65	4.87	6.76
1.750	0.18	1.50	2.07	2.76	3.11	5.28	6.49	8.33
1.775	—	0.88	1.40	2.08	5.40	7.17	8.30	10.11

What effective exchange rates can be guaranteed by hedgers?
What considerations would influence the choice of option series?

Answer

Effective exchange rates include:

Calls	Puts
$1.675 + $0.0524 = $1.7274	$1.675 − $0.015 = $1.660
$1.700 + $0.0362 = $1.7362	$1.700 − $0.0241 = $1.6759

Considerations that influence the choice of option series include:

1. The prices of the alternative option series.
2. The willingness to bear some risk (e.g. using $1.775 calls implies willingness to accept losses of nearly 5 cents/£).
3. The view taken of the currency price movement (a treasurer would not want to pay a large premium for protection against a price rise if a price fall or little change is expected – cheap options such as the $1.775 options would be preferred).
4. Market liquidity – it may be difficult to find sellers of some option series.

Further reading

Jacques P. Pezier and Ravi Viswanathan, *Options* (Woodhead-Faulkner, 1991).

Keith Redhead, *Introduction to Financial Futures and Options* (Woodhead-Faulkner, 1990).

Joseph Walker, *How the Option Market Works* (New York Institute of Finance, 1991).

7

~

Swaps

Currency swaps

The term swap has three different, but related, meanings in the context of international finance:

1. The spot purchase and simultaneous forward sale of a currency.
2. Simultaneous loans in two currencies.
3. The exchange of debt servicing liabilities or the exchange of beneficial ownership of assets.

What follows is concerned with swaps in the third sense. A company, or other body, may wish to exchange a liability in one currency for a liability in another in order to reduce currency exposure. For example, a company with easier access to the UK capital market than to the US market might seek to finance an investment in the US by raising sterling in Britain and selling it for US dollars which are invested in the US. It then has a sterling liability and a US dollar asset. It is vulnerable to a strengthening of sterling against the dollar and would have an interest in swapping its sterling liability for a dollar one.

The currency swap may be carried out by direct negotiation between the counterparties or by means of a bank acting as intermediary and effectively becoming the counterparty to each participant. Figure 7.1 illustrates the latter case. Borrower A acquired a sterling liability and sold the sterling raised for dollars in order to acquire assets in the US. Borrower B, facing easier access to the US capital market than the UK one, borrowed dollars and sold them in order to purchase assets in the UK. Both borrowers have an exchange rate exposure, having assets in one currency and liabilities in another. Borrower A would find that, in the event of a strengthening of the pound against the dollar, both the interest payments and the sum to be repaid at maturity rise in dollar

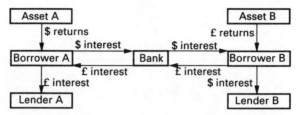

Figure 7.1 Currency swap with a bank as intermediary

value. Conversely, Borrower B is vulnerable to a strengthening of the dollar.

They enter the swap agreements depicted by Figure 7.1. Borrower A simulates a dollar liability whilst Borrower B simulates a sterling liability. This is achieved by means of Borrower A undertaking to meet the interest and principal payments on Borrower B's dollar liability by making the dollar payments to Borrower B via the bank, whilst Borrower B makes a similar commitment to service Borrower A's sterling debt. The bank operates as counterparty to both, and Borrowers A and B need not even know the other's identity. Borrower A remains the debtor of Lender A, similarly for Borrower and Lender B. The lenders may not know of the swap.

The bank runs the risk of losses arising from default by one of the parties. If, for example, the dollar strengthens against sterling, the bank will be gaining from its transactions with Borrower A but losing with B. Normally these gains and losses would cancel each other out but if A were to renege on its obligations, the bank would be left with its loss-making commitments to B. The bank is committed to paying both interest and principal in the relatively strong dollar whilst receiving the same in the weakened sterling.

Swaps allow advantage to be taken of the relatively advantageous terms that some borrowers might obtain in particular markets. In Figure 7.1 Borrower A may be able to borrow sterling more cheaply than Borrower B whilst Borrower B obtains a lower rate of interest than A when borrowing dollars. It is mutually advantageous for both to borrow in their more favorable market and then exchange both the currencies borrowed (in practice, they may buy the desired currency in the spot market rather than exchanging currencies with each other, the effect is the same) and the liabilities acquired. Swaps may arise from different motives and need not involve an exchange of spot currency, there may merely be an agreement to service each other's debt.

Currency swaps

Variations in the terms on which different borrowers can obtain funds in particular currencies can arise for a number of reasons. Exchange controls may inhibit borrowing by non-nationals, a company may be little known outside its own country and hence may have a low credit rating in foreign capital markets, or a market may be saturated with a particular borrower's debt. This latter situation is illustrated by the World Bank's borrowing of Swiss francs in the early 1980s. The Swiss franc market was so saturated with World Bank debt that the Bank was faced with increasing interest rates. It circumvented this problem by borrowing dollars and entering a swap with IBM. There were relatively few US corporates borrowing Swiss francs so such corporates could borrow them at relatively low interest rates. IBM could thus borrow Swiss francs more cheaply than the World Bank. Thus IBM borrowed Swiss francs and entered a Swiss franc/US dollar swap with the World Bank to their mutual advantage.

The forward premium or discount is implicit in the interest flows. Different rates of interest on the two currencies have the same effect as a forward premium/discount. So although the exchange of principal upon maturity of the swap takes place at the same exchange rate as the original exchange of principal the interest rate differential renders the swap equivalent to the use of forward currency contracts.

POSITION TAKING

If borrowers expect that the currency in which their liability is denominated is likely to appreciate they may swap into a currency that they expect to depreciate. If the expected exchange rate movements occur they may subsequently reverse the swap in order to lock in the fall in the value of the liability caused by the exchange rate depreciation.

Figure 7.2 illustrates the case of a borrower with a sterling liability and Deutschmark assets. A borrows sterling which is used to buy

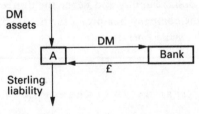

Figure 7.2 Locking in a currency gain

127

Deutschmarks for the purpose of investment in Deutschmark-denominated assets. Following a depreciation of sterling against the Deutschmark, A decides to lock in the gain by swapping the sterling liability for a Deutschmark one. This liability is less than would have been incurred if Deutschmarks had originally been borrowed to finance the acquisition of the Deutschmark asset.

Case study

Locking in a currency gain
A leading British brewing group decided that there was a market for its beer in North America and built a brewery in California. To avoid currency exposure the brewery was financed by borrowing US $100 million.

The sterling–dollar exchange rate had been fairly stable at about £1 = $1.50 for several months when a political crisis in the US caused the dollar to fall to £1 = $1.65. The treasurer of the parent company felt that there was no change in the underlying economic conditions to warrant a dollar depreciation and hence felt that the dollar's decline would be only temporary. He decided to lock in the fall in the sterling value of the dollar liability by entering a currency swap. The dollar liability was swapped for a sterling liability at the exchange rate of £1 = $1.65.

About six months later the political crisis subsided and the exchange rate returned to £1 = $1.50, which was the rate suggested by the principle of purchasing power parity. The treasurer, wanting to again cover the dollar asset exposure, undertook another swap. The sterling liability was swapped for a dollar liability.

At the end of the operation the US dollar liability was about 9% less than it had been at the beginning. The US $100 million debt had been swapped into a £60,606,601 liability and then the £60,606,601 debt had been swapped for a US $90,909,091 liability.

To restore the dollar liability and hence the degree of currency cover to $100 million, the company borrows a further US $9,090,909 which is the profit from the swap operations.

ASSET-BASED CURRENCY SWAPS

Although swaps are typically exchanges of liabilities, the technique can also be used for assets. Figure 7.3 illustrates the situation in which the

Interest rate swaps

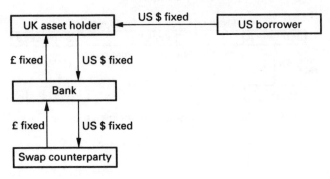

Figure 7.3 Asset-based swap

UK holder of a US dollar bond fears a depreciation of the US dollar against sterling and decides to swap the dollar asset into a sterling asset. The bond-holder receives a flow of interest receipts plus the payment of principal at maturity in US dollars from the US issuer of the bond. Fearing a fall in the value of the dollar the bond-holder swaps into a sterling asset agreeing to pay interest and principal in dollars in return for sterling receipts. The swap counterparty is not necessarily transacting an asset-based swap – either assets or liabilities could be being swapped.

Interest rate swaps

Liabilities denominated in the same currency can effectively be exchanged by means of swaps. This would commonly be for the purpose of changing the basis upon which interest is charged, for example, from a floating rate to a fixed rate basis.

HEDGING INTEREST RISK

Floating rate loans expose the debtor to the risk of increases in the interest rate. A debtor may wish to avoid this risk by taking out a fixed rate loan but, owing to insufficient credit standing, is unable to borrow at fixed rates or can only do so at a particularly high rate of interest. The borrower could attempt to swap the floating rate liability for a fixed rate liability, thereby obtaining fixed rate funds.

The swap may be carried out directly between the two liability holders or may involve a bank as intermediary. In the latter case, the bank might take the role of counterparty to both participants thereby bearing the risk of default by either party and eliminating the need for the participants to investigate the creditworthiness of the other. This has the additional

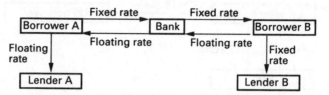

Figure 7.4 Interest rate swap with a bank as intermediary

advantage of allowing anonymity of the parties. It also facilitates swapping by debtors of relatively low creditworthiness.

Figure 7.4 illustrates a case in which a bank operates as intermediary. Borrower A has taken a loan from Lender A at a floating rate of interest but would prefer the certainty provided by a fixed rate loan, and is willing to pay a premium for that certainty. The bank agrees that, in return for the premium, it will provide Borrower A with the funds required to pay the interest on the floating rate loan and accept interest payments at a fixed rate. Lender A is unaffected, their debtor continues to be Borrower A and interest payments continue to be received from that source. Lender A need never know that the swap has taken place. Meanwhile, Borrower A has simulated a fixed rate liability.

The bank seeks to match its commitment by finding a fixed rate borrower wanting a floating rate loan. Borrower B simulates a floating rate loan whilst Lender B retains both fixed rate receipts and the original debtor. If the bank is unable to find a Borrower B that can be matched with Borrower A it may take over the role itself. The bank would thus borrow at a fixed rate and swap its liability with Borrower A. The bank effectively converts its debt from a fixed rate into a floating rate, whilst Borrower A converts it from a floating rate into a fixed rate.

When acting as counterparty to both borrowers, whether or not it has taken the role of Borrower B, the bank faces the risk that a borrower could default. This leaves the bank exposed to an interest rate risk; the remaining customer may be receiving a high rate of interest and paying a low one. The original matching allowed losses from transactions with one customer to be offset by the corresponding gains from the deal with the other customer. Once one of the two counterparties defaults the bank is exposed to the possibility of losses, and indeed the customer from whom the bank is making gains is the one most likely to renege on its agreement.

Case studies

1. A construction company embarks on a private house-building project for which it raises £2,000,000 working capital. Interest is payable on a floating rate basis. Prospective profit margins are tight and could be erased by a substantial increase in interest rates on the loan. The company anticipates that the project will take two years and takes out a two-year fixed for floating swap with a bank. The bank is prepared to act as counterparty and undertakes to meet the floating rate interest payments of the company in return for a fixed rate of 12% p.a. There would be a cash flow between the company and the bank to reflect the difference between the two interest rates.

   The interest rate on the floating rate debt is determined at the beginning of each quarter and paid at the end of the quarter. The resulting cash flows are shown in Table 7.1.

Table 7.1 Cash flows resulting from the swap agreement (from company to bank)

Quarter	Floating rate interest payments	Fixed rate interest payments	Cash flow from company to bank
	£	£	£
1	52,867	57,475	4,608
2	52,867	57,475	4,608
3	52,867	57,475	4,608
4	57,475	57,475	0
5	57,475	57,475	0
6	62,052	57,475	−4,577
7	66,599	57,475	−9,124
8	66,599	57,475	−9,124
			−9,001

Interest rates on the floating rate loan rise progressively from 11% p.a. to 14% p.a. The construction company initially makes payments to the bank but towards the end of the period receives cash flows from the bank. The cash flows between the company and the bank offset the fluctuations in interest rate on the floating rate loan so as to produce a constant quarterly net payment of £57,475.

(Note that the construction company raises a loan from one bank and enters a swap agreement with another bank. A treasurer should not assume that one bank will satisfy all the requirements.)

2. A building society raises £5,000,000 by issuing a eurobond at a fixed interest rate of 11% p.a. over two years, payable six-monthly, for the purpose of providing mortgages on a floating rate basis. It is exposed to the risk that interest rates might fall with the effect that interest receipts from the mortgages are inadequate to meet the interest payments on the eurobond. The building society could eliminate its exposure by swapping its fixed rate liability for one on a floating rate basis. It finds a bank prepared to enter a floating for fixed swap on the basis of receiving LIBOR $+\frac{3}{4}$% p.a. in exchange for paying 11% p.a. Initially LIBOR stands at $10\frac{1}{4}$% p.a. Interest payments to the bank under the swap arrangement, as shown in Table 7.2, are on a six-monthly basis.

LIBOR rises by 0.5% between the first and second years with the result that the building society makes a net payment of £23,702 to the bank.

Table 7.2 Cash flows resulting from the swap agreement (from building society to bank)

Period	Floating rate interest payments	Fixed rate interest payments	Cash flow from building society to bank
	£	£	£
1	267,827	267,827	0
2	267,827	267,827	0
3	279,678	267,827	11,851
4	279,678	267,827	11,851
			23,702

This example underlines the fact that a hedger could either gain or lose from the hedging instrument used. The essential point of hedging is that the gains/losses offset losses/gains on the positions being hedged. In this case the gain from higher mortgage receipts, arising from higher mortgage interest rates, is offset by a loss on the swap. If interest rates had fallen, thereby reducing mortgage interest receipts, there would have been an offsetting gain from the swap.

USING SWAPS TO REDUCE INTEREST COSTS

Investors in fixed rate instruments tend to be more sensitive to differences in creditworthiness than the banks lending on a floating rate basis. In

Interest rate swaps

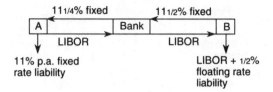

Figure 7.5 Using a swap to exploit comparative advantage

consequence, borrowers of relatively low creditworthiness face a higher interest rate differential in the fixed rate than in the floating rate market. Such borrowers stand to gain by borrowing on a floating rate basis and then swapping into a fixed rate basis with a borrower of higher credit standing. Suppose that Borrower A, with a high credit standing, and Borrower B, with a lower one, face the following interest charges:

	Borrower A	*Borrower B*	*Interest differential*
Floating rate	LIBOR $+\frac{1}{4}$%	LIBOR $+\frac{1}{2}$%	$\frac{1}{4}$%
Fixed rate	11% p.a.	$12\frac{1}{2}$% p.a.	$1\frac{1}{2}$%

The difference in credit standing causes different interest rate differentials in the two markets. If Borrower A wanted floating rate funds and Borrower B needed fixed rate funds, each could reduce interest costs by borrowing in the market in which it had the comparative advantage and then swapping its liability. This is illustrated by Figure 7.5 where the difference between the two interest differentials is $1\frac{1}{4}$% and this is shared between the three participants in the swap transaction. Borrower A receives $11\frac{1}{4}$% p.a. fixed whilst paying 11% p.a. fixed to its creditor plus LIBOR to the intermediating bank. The net outcome for A is a floating rate liability at LIBOR minus $\frac{1}{4}$%. This represents a gain of $\frac{1}{2}$% p.a. relative to borrowing floating rate funds at LIBOR plus $\frac{1}{4}$%. Borrower B receives LIBOR whilst paying LIBOR plus $\frac{1}{2}$% to its creditor and $11\frac{1}{2}$% p.a. fixed to the bank. The net effect is equivalent to paying 12% p.a. fixed, which represents a $\frac{1}{2}$% gain relative to the alternative of borrowing at a fixed rate of $12\frac{1}{2}$% p.a. The intermediary bank receives $11\frac{1}{2}$% p.a. fixed and pays $11\frac{1}{4}$% p.a. fixed thus making a net $\frac{1}{4}$% p.a. in payment for arranging the swap.

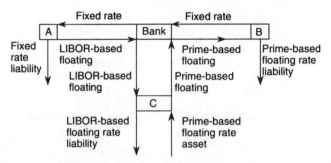

Figure 7.6 Basis swaps – a three-party transaction

BASIS SWAPS

A basis swap is the conversion of a floating rate liability into a floating rate liability with a different rate-setting mechanism. There are a number of alternatives upon which floating rates may be based such as LIBOR, prime, commercial paper and treasury bill rates. Basis swaps can be used to ensure that the floating rates on assets and liabilities are determined on the same basis.

Although these swaps may be established by means of finding two counterparties with equal and opposite requirements they may be three-party arrangements.

Figure 7.6 illustrates such a three-party transaction. Party C transacts a basis swap with two counterparties, each of which undertakes a fixed/floating swap. Party C is able to match the interest basis of its liability to that of its asset because of a mismatch between A and B in relation to their floating rate basis. The LIBOR-based liability of Party C is serviced with interest receipts from A whilst C uses receipts from its prime-based asset to service the liability of B.

CROSS-CURRENCY INTEREST RATE SWAPS (CURRENCY COUPON SWAPS)

These swaps involve changing the currency of denomination as well as the mode of funding, and may involve two, three or more parties. Figure 7.7 illustrates a two-party transaction. Borrower A swaps a fixed rate Deutschmark liability for a floating rate US dollar liability with Borrower B. There may or may not be a simultaneous exchange of currencies with A providing Deutschmarks in exchange for US dollars. Figure 7.8

Zero coupon swaps

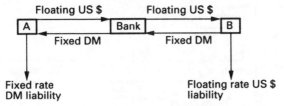

Figure 7.7 Cross-currency interest rate swaps – a two-party transaction

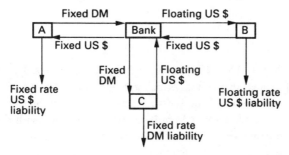

Figure 7.8 Cross-currency interest rate swaps – a three-party transaction

illustrates a three-party swap. Borrower C undertakes a cross-currency interest rate swap whilst Borrower A enters a simple currency swap and Borrower B a simple interest rate swap.

Zero coupon swaps

A zero coupon bond consists of an obligation by the issuer to repay the face value on a specified future date. There are no interest payments and the return to the holder is obtained through purchasing the bond at a discount. For example, a £50 million bond due to mature in ten years might sell at £17 million, thereby implying an 11% p.a. rate of return on the £17 million.

Such a zero coupon bond is equivalent to a bond with a fixed rate of return. The issuer of such a bond could swap the funding to a floating rate basis by simultaneously undertaking an interest rate swap and a reverse annuity. This is illustrated by Figure 7.9. The borrower issues a bond with a face value of £50 million, which is payable at maturity in ten years. The sum received is £17 million which implies that the £50 million has been discounted at 11% p.a. The borrower enters a fixed/floating swap with a counterparty, agreeing to pay LIBOR whilst receiving

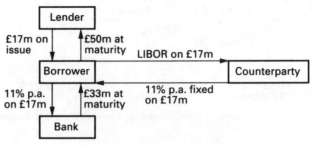

Figure 7.9 Zero coupon swap

a fixed 11% p.a. The 11% p.a. on £17 million is invested with a bank, or other financial institution, which agrees to pay 11% p.a. on the sums invested. At the end of the ten-year term the money invested with the bank has accumulated to £33 million, which together with the original £17 million provides the £50 million payable at the maturity of the zero coupon bond.

Position taking

A swap can be entered into in an attempt to gain from an expected change in interest rates. A holder of a fixed rate liability may swap into a floating rate liability if interest rates are expected to fall. A floating rate liability would provide the opportunity to gain from a fall in interest rates. If interest rates do fall as expected, the floating rate liability might be swapped back into a fixed rate in order to lock in the lower interest rate.

Option swaps (swaptions)

An option swap gives the right, but not the obligation, to enter into a swap during a specified period on terms agreed at the time of entering the option. When swapping from floating to fixed, the fixed rate agreed may be a specific percentage or may be related to the rate on a particular financial instrument. For example, the option may provide the right to swap into a fixed rate borrowing at 12% p.a. or alternatively, it may specify 50 basis points above Treasury $15\frac{1}{2}$% 1998. In the case of swaps into floating rates a particular relationship with a rate will be agreed, for example, 80 basis points above LIBOR. The profile of an option swap might be the following:

Warehousing

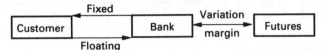

Figure 7.10 Warehousing with futures

Duration of option: 6 months
Notional volume: £25,000,000
Maturity from exercise: 5 years
Fixed rate: 12% p.a.
Variable rate: LIBOR $+\frac{1}{2}$%
Option premium: £250,000

The option holder thus acquires the right to swap a £25,000,000 floating rate borrowing into a fixed one at 12% p.a. at any time during the next six months at a cost of a premium of £250,000. If rates rise above 12% p.a. the option can be profitably exercised, but if rates fall so that it becomes possible to swap into a lower fixed rate, then the option will not be exercised. By paying the premium the borrower is insured against having to pay more than 12% p.a. when swapping a floating rate debt into a fixed rate one.

A variation on the theme is the timing option. This differs from a normal option in that the option holder is obliged to enter into the swap during the specified period. The choice relates solely to the timing of the exercise of the option.

Warehousing

Warehousing by a bank consists of doing a swap and hedging it. When a suitable swap counterparty appears the hedge is undone. One way in which the hedging might be carried out is by the use of financial futures. For example, a bank might agree to pay fixed against receiving floating and covers the risk of a fall in interest rates by buying financial futures (see Figure 7.10).

By buying three-month interest rate futures contracts the bank can lock in interest rates. If interest rates fall the price of futures contracts will rise providing the bank with a gain that compensates for the interest rate fall.

The willingness to make a market in swaps has considerably increased the speed with which swaps are provided. Deals are available on demand without requiring simultaneous availability of a matching counterparty.

Case study

Warehousing a swap

A deutschmark swaps market maker provides a $\frac{3}{12}$ swap in which a fixed twelve-month payment of 5.50% is guaranteed in return for a three-month floating receipt (LIBOR). The swap has a maturity of one year. The market maker is exposed to a fall in interest rates, and thus takes a futures position that would profit from a fall in interest rates (rise in futures prices). Futures contracts are purchased.

Data on 18th September

Size of swap	DM10 million
Twelve-month fixed rate	5.50%
Spot three-month LIBOR	5.53%
Futures prices – December	94.49
– March	94.67
– June	94.69

Action taken on 18th September

Buy a strip. At DM1 million per contract this involves:
10 December, 10 March and 10 June futures contracts.

Target interest rate

Since the starting date is 18th September the three interest rollover dates would coincide with, or be very close to, the futures maturity dates. The rates of interest implied by spot LIBOR and the three futures prices are 5.53% p.a., 5.51% p.a., 5.33% p.a. and 5.31% p.a., respectively. Dividing by four in order to obtain the three-month rates and compounding yields:

$$[1.013\,825 \times 1.013\,775 \times 1.013\,325 \times 1.013\,275] - 1 = 0.055\,3114$$

i.e. 5.53% p.a.

Asset-based interest rate swaps

An interest rate swap could be used by a fixed rate bond-holder to gain from a rise in interest rates. Figure 7.11 depicts the situation in which the holder of a bond with a coupon yield of 12% p.a. feels that interest rates, now at 10% p.a. for maturities matching the remaining term of

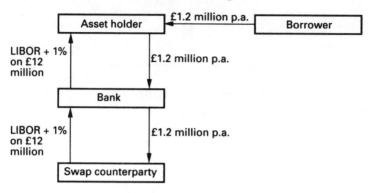

Figure 7.11 Asset-based swap

the bond, are likely to rise. He swaps into a floating rate asset in order to profit from a rise in interest rates.

The lender originally buys an undated bond for £10 million at 12% p.a. When the interest rate on undated debt falls to 10% p.a. the value of the bond rises to £12 million. By swapping the fixed coupon yield of £1.2 million p.a. for LIBOR + 1% on £12 million, the lender obtains the opportunity to profit from a rise in interest rates. The lender could reverse the swap (by entering another swap) subsequent to a rise in interest rates to fix a rate on £12 million so that at the end of the operation the annual receipts are in excess of £1.2 million p.a.

Further reading

Boris Antl, *Swap Financing Techniques* (Euromoney, 1983).
Michael Z. Brooke, *Handbook of International Financial Management* (Macmillan, 1990).
Sherree DeCovny, *Swaps* (Woodhead-Faulkner 1992).

8

~

Future developments

A number of current trends in the international money markets seem set to continue. Further development can be expected along a number of lines including globalization, electronic trading, international regulation, securitization and basket currency instruments.

Globalization

Securities markets are becoming increasingly international. A particular stock or bond may be traded on the markets of several different countries. Some companies have sought to widen the foreign ownership of their stock by making international share offerings. Portfolios have, correspondingly, become more international in terms of both stocks and bonds. Increased internationalization adds to diversification and hence lowers risk for any particular rate of return.

Within Europe, progress towards economic and monetary union could lead some investors to regard the members of the European Communities as constituting a single investment market. Such a tendency is supported by the increasing frequency of bond issues denominated in European Currency Units (ECUs). Europe already has an active international market place for the trading of stocks and bonds from throughout Europe in the form of the London stock market.

However, it is to be expected that, for some time to come, stock markets will remain fragmented in the sense of many stocks being traded only on the domestic stock markets. Many investors prefer markets to be fragmented and inefficient since such markets offer profit opportunities. However, as outsiders enter inefficient markets in pursuit of profits they will help to develop those markets and reduce their inefficiencies.

Regulation

Electronic trading

The development of electronic trading is closely tied with the globalization of markets. Existing exchanges are extending their trading hours in order to compete with markets in different time zones and are using screen-based electronic trading for the additional periods. North American exchanges are aiming to trade throughout the European trading day. It might be merely a matter of time before 24-hour trading becomes the norm. It could also be merely a matter of time before the electronic systems used for the additional hours take over the normal trading hours from the floor traders. In other words, markets could become entirely screen-based electronic systems disembodied from trading floors.

Such developments are true not only of stock exchanges, but also of derivatives exchanges. The world's two biggest futures exchanges, the Chicago Board of Trade and the Chicago Mercantile Exchange, together with Reuters have been developing a worldwide electronic trading system known as Globex. It is envisaged that this system will operate globally on a 24-hour basis. US options exchanges are also engaged in developing a worldwide electronic trading system. The Chicago Board Options Exchange, the American Stock Exchange and the Cincinnati Stock Exchange are together seeking to develop a system.

Regulation

The globalization of markets is bringing a number of regulatory issues to the fore. There seems to be general agreement on the need to achieve greater international co-ordination with regard to the regulation of securities markets and securities market intermediaries. Two dimensions of this that have been the subject of multilateral approaches are those of achieving a common standard of capital adequacy for securities firms and the world wide upgrading of settlement systems.

A common standard of capital adequacy has already been agreed for banks. The requirements are known as the Basle guidelines. They stipulate a minimum ratio of capital to assets of 8%. In this context it is interesting to note that in a number of countries, including the United States and Japan, initiatives have been launched with a view to ending the division between the banking and securities industries.

Future developments

Securitization

Securitization involves repackaging existing assets as bonds and then selling them. The asset that has most often been used as the basis for securitization is the mortgage. Mortgage lenders can issue bonds that are backed by mortgages. By doing this, the mortgage lenders effectively remove the mortgages from their balance sheets and replace them with money when the bonds are sold. Another class of asset against which bonds have been issued has been the credit card receivable. In effect, the buyer of the bonds becomes the beneficiary of the credit card repayments.

Securitization is much more advanced in the United States than elsewhere. However, the practice can be expected to spread globally. One aspect holding back its development is its high cost, especially for first-time issuers. These costs stem from both the need to establish systems to handle the underlying assets and the need to straighten out potential legal complications.

Basket currencies

Probably the basket with the greatest impact thus far is the European Currency Unit (ECU). At the time of writing, bonds denominated in ECUs had become the second most active currency sector in the eurobond market. Issuers have included national governments as well as private corporations. Corresponding to the growth of ECU-denominated eurobond issuance and trading two futures exchanges, the London International Financial Futures and Options Exchange and the MATIF in Paris, have introduced ECU bond futures contracts.

The ECU has also made an impact at the shorter end of the maturity spectrum. Interbank deposits range from overnight to twelve months and certificates of deposit in ECUs are sold by major banks. Also some governments, notably those of the United Kingdom and Italy, have made ECU-denominated treasury bill issues. Correspondingly there are derivatives based on short-term ECU-denominated instruments. The London Derivatives Exchange has a three-month ECU interest rate futures contract. There are also forward rate agreements in ECUs.

Increasing European economic and monetary integration might be expected to strengthen this trend. Perhaps other basket currencies, such as Special Drawing Rights, might, in time, show a similar impact on the international money markets.

Glossary

Acceptance   By accepting a bill issued by a company a bank guarantees that it will be honoured.

Arbitrage   Exploiting price anomalies for profit. For example, if prices for the same item differ between locations the item may be bought relatively cheaply and sold at a higher price. Pure arbitrage involves no risk and no use of the arbitrager's own capital.

Ask price   The price at which an investor can buy.

Bank bill   A bill of exchange accepted by a bank.

Basis point   1/100th of 1%

Bear   Someone who expects a fall in the prices of instruments such as stocks and bonds.

Bearer bond   A bond that is not registered in a name. The rights to coupons and principal accrue to the holder.

Beta   A measure of the responsiveness of the price of an individual stock to movements in stock prices as a whole.

Bid price   The price at which an investor can sell to a market maker.

Bid rate   The rate of interest at which an investor can deposit money.

Bill of Exchange   A document which commits one company to pay a specific sum of money to another on a particular date.

Bond   A security sold in order to raise capital. Bonds normally provide the buyer with an income flow plus the return of the initial capital on the maturity date of the bond.

Broker   An intermediary that buys or sells on behalf of an investor or other client.

Broker-dealer   A broker that can deal on their own account as well as acting as an agent for clients.

Bull   Someone who expects a rise in the price of a financial instrument.

Call money   A bank loan repayable on demand.

Call option   The right to buy a financial instrument at a specific price during a period of time (or at a point in time).

Certificate of Deposit   A negotiable instrument issued by a bank in return for a deposit. The maturity is normally short, for example, three months.

Circuit breaker   Price change limits and trading halts aimed at curbing the extent of price fluctuations.

Glossary

Clearing house An institution that settles mutual indebtedness between organizations or which records trades (in the case of futures and options the clearing house may also become the counterparty to contract holders).

Commercial bill A bill issued by an organization other than a government.

Commercial paper Unsecured notes issued by companies for short-term borrowing.

Convertible bond A bond that can be converted into a specified number of shares of stock at a point, or points, in time.

Coupon An interest payment on a bond or note.

Currency account Bank account in a foreign currency.

Direct quotation Quotation of an exchange rate in terms of a number of units of the domestic currency per unit of the foreign currency.

Discount 1. Amount by which the current price falls below the final redemption value of a security. 2. Amount by which the forward price of a currency falls below its spot price.

Discount rate The rate of interest used to convert a future value into a present value.

Disintermediation Flows of funds between borrowers and lenders (e.g. by bond sales) that do not involve the money passing through financial intermediaries such as banks.

Dividends The payments by a company to its shareholders (owners of ordinary shares or common stock).

Drop-lock bond A floating rate bond which automatically becomes a fixed rate bond in the event of interest rates falling below a particular level.

ECU European Currency Unit. A basket currency comprising sums of the currencies of the members of the European Monetary System (EMS).

Eurobond A bond issued in a currency other than that of the country in which the bond is issued.

Eurocurrency Deposits and loans denominated in a currency other than that of the country in which the deposit is held or loan made.

European Monetary System (EMS) A system of stable exchange rates between members of the European Communities.

Exercise price The price at which the holder of an option has the right to buy or sell (alternatively known as the strike price).

Financial future The notional right to buy or sell a standard quantity of a financial instrument on a specific future date at a price determined at the time of buying or selling the futures contract.

Fixed interest security A bond that pays a fixed sum of money per year.

Floating rate security A bond, or other security, on which the income payments move in line with the market rates of interest.

Flotation The issue of shares of stock in a company for the first time.

Foreign exchange Foreign currencies that can be used to finance international trade.

Forfaiting The purchase of receivables arising from exports. The forfaiter buys the right to collect money from the foreign importer.

Glossary

Forward Agreement to exchange financial instruments on a future date, e.g. forward currency.

Forward–forward Agreement on the future exchange of financial instruments that will mature on a more distant date, e.g. forward–forward interest rates.

Forward rate agreement (FRA) Notional agreement to deposit or borrow on a specific future date at an interest rate determined in the present (a form of interest rate future).

Fundamental analysis Ascertaining the appropriate prices of securities by analysing economic data.

Gilt Gilt-edged security. A British government bond.

Hard currency A currency that is convertible into major currencies such as the US dollar.

Hedge A transaction undertaken in order to reduce an existing risk.

Indirect quotation Quotation of an exchange rate in terms of the number of units of foreign currency per unit of domestic currency.

Institutional investor An institution that invests money on behalf of a number of smaller investors, e.g. pension fund, insurance fund, mutual fund.

Interbank market The market in which banks lend to, and borrow from, one another.

Intermediary An institution that takes deposits and uses the receipts to make loans.

Intrinsic value The gross profit available from the immediate exercise of an (American-style) option.

Junk bond Corporate bond with high risk of default and corresponding high yield.

Kerb market Unofficial market, often operating outside the normal trading hours of the official market.

LIBOR London Interbank Offer Rate. The rate of interest at which major banks in London will lend to each other.

Liquidity Assets that are either in the form of money or can be easily converted into money.

Market maker A dealer who publishes bid and ask prices on certain securities and is committed to trade at those prices. It is thus ensured that a market always exists in those securities.

Maturity Period to the redemption of a financial claim.

Money broker As a broker in the interbank market, a money broker brings together banks wishing to lend and those wishing to borrow. There are also money brokers in currencies and Eurobonds.

Negative yield curve Short-term interest rates higher than long-term ones.

Normal distribution The distribution of the probabilities of alternative values of a variable (e.g. a price). It has a bell-shaped form indicating high probabilities of values near the average and low probability of extreme values.

Note An instrument recording a promise to pay sums of money in the future. Similar to bonds but typically of shorter maturity.

145

Glossary

Offer price   The price at which an investor can buy.

Offer rate   The rate of interest at which money can be borrowed.

Offshore banking   Banking facilities in locations that offer a very favorable tax environment. Typically the country in which the bank is registered is not that in which the actual banking operations are undertaken.

Open interest   The number of outstanding contracts in a futures market.

Open market operations   Dealings in the money markets by a central bank for the purpose of influencing the liquidity of financial institutions and/or controlling interest rates.

Open outcry   Face-to-face trading (as opposed to screen-based trading).

Option   The right to buy or sell at a specific price during a time period (or at a point in time). Can also be a right to borrow or lend at a particular interest rate.

Over the counter (OTC)   Tailor-made instruments, as opposed to the standardized exchange-traded ones.

Parallel money markets   Markets in short-term securities other than bills and bonds. They encompass Certificates of Deposit and interbank lending (including Eurocurrency transactions).

Positive yield curve   Long-term interest rates higher than short-term ones.

Premium   1. Price of an option.   2. Amount by which the forward price of a currency exceeds its spot price.   3. Excess of a futures value over the spot value.

Price–earnings ratio   The ratio of the price of an ordinary share (common stock) to the earnings (profits) per share of stock.

Principal   1. Someone buying or selling on their own account rather than as an agent for a client.   2. The sum of money repayable at the maturity of a bond or other debt instrument.

Put option   The right to sell an instrument at a particular price during a time period (or on a specific date).

Repo   Sale and repurchase agreement. The sale of short-term securities with a simultaneous commitment to buy them back at a later date. A means of short-term borrowing.

Rescheduling   Rearranging the terms of a loan.

Rights issue   An offer of new shares of stock to existing holders.

Risk management   Controlling the level of financial risk to which an organization is exposed, e.g. by hedging.

SDR   Special Drawing Rights. A form of international money issued by the International Monetary Fund.

Secondary market   A market in which already existing securities are bought and sold. Distinct from the primary market in which newly issued securities are sold.

Securitization   1. The aggregating of existing assets such as mortgages so as to use them as backing for bond issues, effectively selling a bundle of existing assets.   2. Sale of bills or bonds as an alternative to borrowing from banks.

Security   A medium of investment, e.g. stocks, bonds, bills.

146

Glossary

Share   Instrument denoting part ownership of the equity of a company. Alternatively known as a stock.

Short selling   Selling borrowed stock.

Sovereign loan   Bank loan to a government.

Sovereign risk   1. Risk of default on a sovereign loan.   2. Risk of expropriation of assets held in a foreign country.

Speculation   Buying or selling with a view to making profits from price changes.

Spot price   Current price as opposed to forward or futures price.

Spread   The excess of the ask (offer) price or interest rate over the bid price or interest rate. It is the market maker's or banker's margin.

Standard deviation   A measure of the extent to which a set of values (forming a normal distribution) are dispersed around their average (mean). Often used as a measure of price volatility.

Stock   Most commonly used to denote shares representing ownership of the equity of a firm (common stock, ordinary shares). However, it is sometimes treated as synonymous with bonds.

Stock exchange   Market for the trading of stocks and bonds.

Stock index   A measure of the average value of stock prices at a point in time (e.g. S & P 500, FTSE 100, Nikkei Dow, DAX, CAC 40, Hang Seng).

Swap   1. An agreement by two parties to service one another's debts.   2. A simultaneous spot purchase (or sale) and forward sale (or purchase), i.e. buying for one point in time and selling for another.

Technical analysis   Prediction of price movements based on the proposition that markets have their own internal momentum independent of economic events. Chartism is a form of technical analysis that uses charts and graphs of past price movements to forecast future price behaviour.

Treasury bill   A debt instrument issued by the central government for raising short-term finance.

Treasury bond   A debt instrument issued by the central government for raising long-term finance.

Underwrite   To guarantee that the whole issue of a security will be purchased (by the underwriter if necessary).

Unsecured loan   A loan without collateral or charge on the assets of the borrower.

Volatility   A measure of fluctuation. Particularly used in relation to price movements. Frequently measured in terms of the standard deviation or variance of the distribution of prices.

Warrant   A long-term option giving the holder the right to subscribe for a stock (or other instrument) at a specific price during a period of time.

Wholesale market   The market for deposits and loans in which each transaction involves a large sum of money. It is largely an interbank market.

Yield curve   The relationship between the maturity of a security and the rate of return it provides.

Zero coupon bond   A bond that pays no interest or coupon. The return to the holder arises from the bond being sold at a discount to its redemption value at maturity.

Index

Index

Index

Index

Index

ticks, 95
time value of options, 112–13
Tokyo International Financial Futures
    Exchange (TIFFE), 91
Tokyo Stock Exchange (TSE), 91, 92
trade bills, 46
transparent markets, 102
treasury bills, 45–6, 142, 147

United Kingdom, 9, 45, 46–7, 142
United States, 10, 45, 141, 142
    balance of payments deficits, 4, 7, 9–10
    dollar *see* dollar
    Foreign Credit Restraint Program, 5, 6
    gold price, 2, 6
    Interest Equalization Tax, 5, 6
    International Banking Facilities, 5
    Regulation Q, 6
unitizing debt, 66–8

up-and-in put options, 118
up-and-out put options, 118

variance, portfolio, 72–3
variation margin, 93–4

walking stick yield curve, 61, 65
warehousing, 137–8
warrants, 119–20, 147
World Bank, 127

Yankee bonds, 12
yen, 8
yield, measures of, 80–1
yield curves, 60–1, 65, 65–6, 81–3, 147

zero cost options, 110–11
zero coupon swaps, 135–6